ANTIQUES
from the
COUNTRY
Kitchen

Frances Thompson

Cover Design: Geri Wolfe Boesen
Interior Layout: Anthony Jacobson

Photographs by the author

Library of Congress Catalog
Card Number 84-052716

ISBN 0-87069-449-9

10 9 8 7 6 5 4 3 2 1

Published by

Wallace-Homestead Book Company
580 Waters Edge
Lombard, Illinois 60148

One of the
ABC PUBLISHING
Companies

For
Dr. Ann Bailey

Contents

Acknowledgments   5

1 The Kitchen   7

2 Wash on Monday   53

3 Iron on Tuesday   63

4 Bake on Wednesday   75

5 Brew on Thursday   113

6 Churn on Friday   123

7 Mend on Saturday   139

8 Go to Church on Sunday   155

About the Author   162

Acknowledgments

Thanks to Blount Mansion, Knoxville, Tennessee; John Coker, Ltd., New Market, Tennessee; Old North Hull Historical District, Montgomery, Alabama; Pike Pioneer Museum, Troy, Alabama; Bedingfield Inn and Westville, the restored 1850 village, Lumpkin, Georgia; Country Place Antiques, Graceville, Florida; and the hundreds of antiques dealers all over the country who have allowed me to photograph their antiques through the years.

Rock, log, and mud chimney

1

The Kitchen

The fascination for kitchens began in the days of the Colonists, and it has continued as people remember the warmth, aromas, and love found in the kitchens of their childhood.

The kitchen always has been warm, cheerful, and homey—the most interesting room in the home. But the early ones weren't as picturesque as we might imagine. The walls were usually bare and unpainted, the windows small, and the furniture sparse and homemade. But there was a warmth and welcome that made all the difference.

When the Pilgrims arrived in the New World, they had a difficult decision to make. Which was more important—food or shelter? The Pilgrims opted for food, choosing to clear the fields and plant while living in caves for the first year or so. Later arrivals also lived in caves, some for years, while they devoted all their time and energy to clearing and cultivating the land.

Once the crops were planted and the Pilgrims were reasonably certain of having food, they did try to build homes. The entire area was covered with large trees—enough to supply the whole world with lumber, yet the only thing they had to cut the trees were broadaxes. It would be a long time before they would have sawmills. There was no way to make bricks, either, although the raw materials were at hand.

As people spread out across this new land, they built cabins made from the logs they cut to clear the land as they moved westward and southward. The first homes and many of those built later had just one room for eating, sleeping, and living.

The fireplace in such a home was the most important part of the room. Used for heating and cooking, the fireplace usually took up the most of one wall.

During the next century or so, settlers built seats like window seats on either side of the fireplace so the children could sit and study their lessons by the light of the burning fire. In some of the later homes, the seats were replaced by chimney cupboards.

There was usually a new baby in the family, kept in the cradle near the fireplace. Those cradles varied from the crudely hollowed-out log models to the brightly decorated Pennsylvania Dutch examples. The children in those early families grew from babyhood to adulthood without ever leaving the kitchen, except for work and school. It was only natural for them to love the kitchen.

For many generations, the parents slept in the kitchen—even after larger houses were built. In the early days, they slept there for warmth and to keep the fire burning all night—especially in the winter. Two or three of the younger children slept in a trundle bed by the parents' bed. If they took naps during the day, they usually slept in the parents' bed, because the trundle took up too much space when the family was active.

It may seem strange that a fire would be kept burning in summer as well as winter in a fireplace whose chimney was a fire hazard. But it was such a chore to get a fire burning that the pioneers wouldn't let it die out.

Since man first learned he could start a fire with flint and steel, he has tried to keep those essentials around the house. In the New World, it was not always possible. When someone accidentally let the fire go out, the only way to start it again was to send one of the children to the nearest neighbor's cabin with a shovel or covered container to bring back live coals to rekindle the fire.

Swinging cradle

Crude, early cradle

Early hooded cradle

Higher quality hooded cradle

Homemade cradle

Cradle after the Pennsylvania style

As they acquired more of the necessities of life, the Colonists began to keep what they called tinderboxes—usually a round tin box with flint, steel, and tinder. The latter could be any kind of fabric, but was generally an old worn or scorched piece of linen that was saved especially for that purpose. It was used to catch the sparks made by striking the flint and steel. The burning linen was then put into the fireplace near some splinters or kindling, and eventually the fire would begin to burn. It was a time-consuming chore; old-timers say that if you got a fire started in less than an hour, you were lucky.

Those fireplaces were necessary for more than just cooking and warming the house in the winter. Before other types of lighting were available, those fires furnished the only light the family had at night.

For lack of other lighting, the early Colonists reverted to the lighting used by the caveman—the pine knot torch. Pine trees were plentiful and available in every section of the country. All the settlers had to do was gather the trees from the forest, then light them at night. They gave off a rather bright light, but had one distinct disadvantage—the constantly dripping tar that stuck to everything. There was also the problem of the black smoke that filled the room—especially in the winter when the cabin door was closed.

In 1642, one Colonist wrote that he could not recommend the pine tree "candlewood" because "it droppeth a pitchy kind of substance where it stands." But pitchy substance or not, the pine knot or, as it was called in the South, the "litard knot," was used well into the twentieth century. Ingenious settlers discovered early that the pine torches could be placed on a rock in the corner of the fireplace. This eliminated some of the smoke as it went up the chimney, and the tar ended up on the rock, which was then discarded.

For centuries, people walked to their church services at night. Most had to go through wooded areas. They usually walked in groups, with the leader carrying a blazing litard knot that not only lighted their path, but kept wild animals at a distance. This custom continued in some rural areas for many years, even after other types of lighting became available.

Due to the smoke and tar, the pine knot or candlewood type of lighting was discarded for indoor use with the arrival of the blacksmiths, who began making iron grease lamps. The first ones were bowl-shaped on a stem, with a larger iron base to catch the drippings. Betty lamps came next, and differed only in that they were made to hang on the wall, mantel, or back of a chair.

This was a time when the old saying, "Waste not—want not" was treated as gospel. Nobody wasted anything, yet people were not stingy when it came to sharing with a neighbor, as they all knew their survival depended on one another. But when it came to accumulating grease and tallow to be used to make the winter's candle supply, people hoarded their supplies. Candles made a brighter light than either the grease or Betty lamps, and they burned much cleaner. Women began dipping candles as soon as they had enough raw materials.

Records are skimpy on the exact date the first ready-made candles were shipped to the Colonies, but it is known that in the early 1600s, when Governor Winthrop sent his wife a list of things to bring when she sailed from England, candles were on the list. Apparently, the cost of four-pence each made candles a luxury. Later, the Winthrops made their own with wicks and tallow shipped from England.

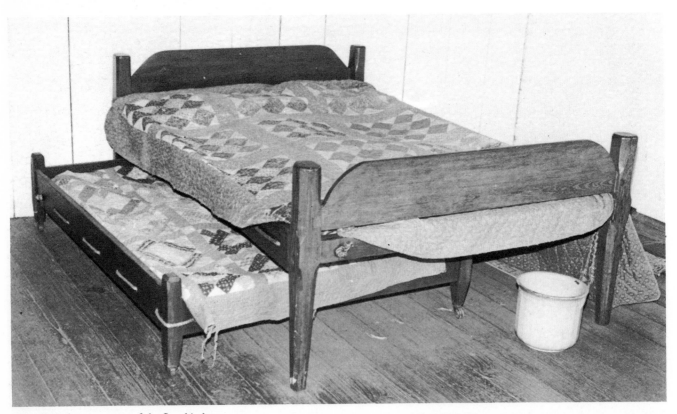

Trundle beds were a part of the first kitchens

Settlers made wicks out of loosely spun hemp, tow, or cotton. Later they made a better candle using beeswax. Bayberry was perhaps the most often used candle material in New England, simply because it was so plentiful and easy to obtain. In the early days, the berries were known by various names— depending on who was picking and using them. The Swedes called the plant the tallow-shrub, while the English dubbed it the candle-berry or bayberry bush. Since the berries were free for the taking, the housewife no longer had to be stingy with her grease and tallow. But apparently some people abused the privilege and destroyed the bushes as they picked the berries. In some towns, a law was passed forbidding the harvesting of bayberries before a certain date. This was the beginning of the poachers—in this case, berry poachers.

The Colonists used whatever materials they had that would make a reasonably good candle. Later, they added extra ingredients to make prettier candles, or ones that burned brighter or longer. Lists of the ingredients of those early candles were probably never written down; instead, they were passed from one generation to the next by word of mouth. After all, the Colonists

Early grease lamp

Later trundle bed, which might have also been in the kitchen

Late Betty lamp

11

Three-candle mold

Eight-candle mold

were ingenious, inventive people who didn't hesitate to try something new. They could afford to experiment, as most of their raw materials were obtained free from the fields, forest, and streams. All they invested was time.

Around 1860, people followed these candlemaking instructions: Take two pounds of alum for every ten pounds of tallow. Dissolve the alum in water before the tallow is put in, and then melt the tallow in the alum water, with frequent stirring, and it will clarify and harden the tallow so as to make a most beautiful candle for either winter or summer use. In lighting candles always hold the light to the side of the wick, not over the top.

This was probably aimed at the southern housewife, as the heat would have melted the average candle in the summer.

It was during this heyday of the candle that the candle mold came into use. Usually made of tin, it might have held three or four candles at a time. Or, as a larger standing mold, it could have made two dozen or more candles at once. The making of the candle molds furnished work for the tinsmith while another new trade was created through the candles themselves—the itinerant candlemakers who went from house to house making the family's winter supply of candles. Many housewives continued to make their own candles, but the candlemakers had plenty of work with the more affluent families.

Other candle-related gadgets also came into use. First, there was the candle box, which was stored in a cabinet, on the mantel, on a table, or hung in the house. It might be made of tin or wood, but its purpose was to protect the candles. Another necessary tool was the candle snuffer. Many of the early ones were made of iron, but later they would be made of silver with matching trays.

All progress made in the early days of the Colonies is interesting, but none is more so than the progress of light. Fishermen discovered whale oil that could be used to supply light when burned in metal or glass lamps. The public was delighted, and some of the fishermen became wealthy selling whale oil. For those unable to afford the oil, cheap though it might have been, there was an alternative—spermaceti, a material found in the heads of the whales. Candles made with spermaceti had larger flames than the combined flames of four tallow candles, and they gave more light than the combined light of three tallow candles.

Eventually, some planters, shippers, and merchants were rich enough to build large houses that required lighting in several rooms at the same time. This in turn necessitated the use of candle holders. Some were small so they could be carried upstairs at night when the family retired. And for the dining room there was the chandelier, made of tin or wood, that would hold nearly a dozen candles. Candle holders ran the gamut from the iron examples made by the local blacksmith to the ornate brass and silver ones shipped from England. In between were the tin candle holders and sconces made by the tinsmith, the pottery examples, and the glass ones.

Later there would be the kerosene lamps, and eventually electricity. In the meantime, the size of the homes continued to grow. The houses were filled with exquisite lamps, cut and art glass lamps, and later the finest of them all, Tiffany lamps.

On the frontier, though, cabins were improving slowly but surely. Growing families sometimes added a room on the other side of the chimney so the fire could heat both rooms. The first cabins were built around a stump left from cutting the logs, which then served as a table. Slowly the pioneers acquired real tables for dining. By most standards they were rather crude, but they showed progress.

One of the most needed and biggest improvements was replacing the log and mud chimney with stone. While the fire was out and the work in progress, settlers added an oven to the side of the new fireplace to be used for baking breads, biscuits, and maybe a pie or two. It was easy enough to cook a large covered skillet or Dutch oven full of biscuits or cornbread in coals on the hearth. But an oven could cook fancier foods.

Four- and twelve-candle molds

Twenty-four candle mold

Wooden candle box

Pair of brass candle holders

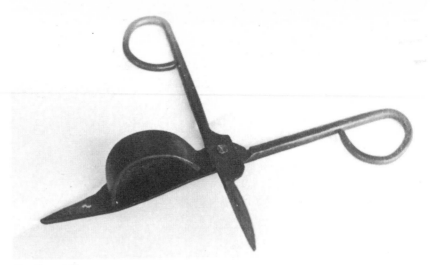

Candle snuffer

Round-based brass candle holders

Miniature brass candle holders

Rock or stone chimney on log cabin

Cooking was done in some fireplaces

Fireplace with two cranes

Iron gridiron or trivet

Spit hung in front of fire to cook or roast meat

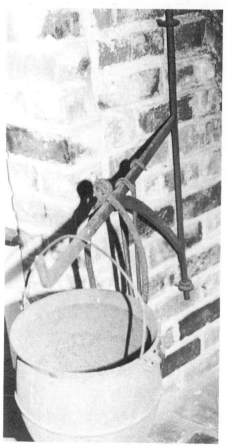
Close-up of crane

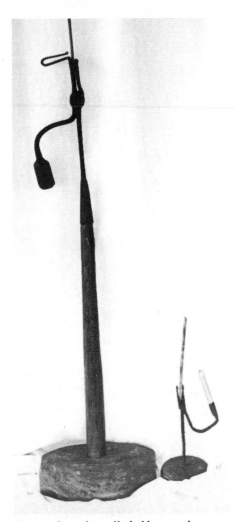

Iron and wood candle holders, early

Settlers added gridirons or large, rotating trivets made by the local black-smith, which held pots of food that needed to be cooked slowly as the pot rotated by the fire. It was also easier to ladle out the food when it was on the gridiron or trivet than when it was on the crane or trammel over the blaz-ing fire.

At first, little storage space had been needed, as settlers had little to store. Extra food was kept in holes dug in the ground, while the foods that required drying, such as beans, apples, herbs, and others were hung around the walls of the kitchen. This, of course, accounted for part of the heavenly aroma associated with early kitchens.

Another improvement in the kitchen was the addition of a mantel, often called a mantel shelf, over the fireplace. Later, settlers would add a valance made of fabric and a shelf clock. Prior to that time, they were liable to put anything on the mantel, such as the Betty lamp, the candle molds, or a tin candle holder complete with candle. In some of the homes, there might be a tin sconce on either side of the mantel and a tin candle holder on the mantel proper.

In the early days pioneers made a bench-type arrangement on one side of the cabin wall to serve as a bed. That was an improvement over the leaves and small boughs from trees that had made beds on the dirt floor.

Later, some settlers devised what they called the "turn-up" bed, with boards nailed together and hinged on the wall. It could be let down at night for sleeping and turned up against the wall during the day. Since most of the cabin space was needed during the day for cooking and eating, this was a satis-factory arrangement. The turn-up bed seems to have been the forerunner of the Murphy bed.

Pioneers devised another type of bed that was only a frame resting on two stumps, and was brought into the cabin each night. In some cases, the stumps may have remained in the house during the day to serve as stools or backless chairs. The frame, which could be propped against the wall during the day, was a network of ropes, much like the later rope beds that held mattresses.

Adults continued to sleep in the kitchen long after the houses were enlarged, but as soon as possible they acquired a rope bed or one with a valance or curtains, as the winters in New England could be extremely cold.

The children who slept in the lofts or other rooms are said to have suffered from the cold, as the heat from the old fireplaces only reached three

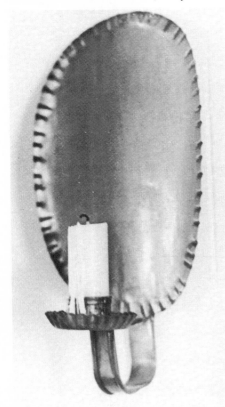

Tin sconce

Old fireplace with candle molds on mantel

16

or four feet from the burning logs. Several of the early settlers—those who could read and write—kept diaries or records of the happenings in their areas. Cotton Mather once wrote that it was impossible for him and others in his area to keep their diaries current in winter, as the ink would freeze before they could complete a sentence.

There was no prepared ink; each person made his own. Unfortunately, settlers must have thought this was a mundane thing, for they didn't leave a recipe. Later, in the 1850s, indelible ink was made by mixing "six cents worth of lunar caustic; one drachm of salt of tartar; and one quarter of an ounce of gum Arabic."

To make brilliant black ink it was necessary to mix "a quarter of a pound of extract of logwood; one gallon of rain water; heat to boiling point in an iron kettle; skim well and stir; then add ninety grains of bichromate potash; fifteen grains of prussiate potash, dissolve in half a pint of the hot water. Stir for three minutes, take off and drain." Even if the ingredients could be found today, we do not recommend them, nor do we know if they are workable.

Then, as now, there were problems with ink stains. To extract durable ink, "rub the ink stain with a little sal-ammonia moistened with water." There was also a recipe for sand soap that was said to be invaluable for taking ink spots off one's hands. It was made by adding sand to a pint of cooling lye soap. It was then made into "cakes," as bars of soap were called then, and put out to dry. It was also recommended for cleaning tinware and grease spots. "Tinware," settlers said, "passed through such suds is cleansed and polished by the process, and wash basins and other pieces may be rinsed after and look well."

Some of the experiences of Mrs. Winthrop, wife of the governor, can be used to show how primitive living conditions were in the Colonies in the early days. They also show that, regardless of your station in life, you still had to put up with the inconveniences. Upon her arrival in the Colonies in 1631, Mrs. Winthrop began doing her chores just like the other wives. She cooked the meals, baking her own bread, and she carried water from a spring down the road from their home.

She was not alone when she carried the heavy buckets of water. Everybody had to walk to the nearest stream to find water used for drinking, cleaning, and bathing. This might explain why it was quite a while before they decided cleanliness was next to godliness.

The chore of carrying wooden buckets of water from the nearest stream was the inspiration for the shoulder yoke—the long wooden yoke seen sometimes in antiques shows and shops. The fact that yokes were used over a long period accounts for their availability now. The wooden yoke was whittled out to fit across a person's shoulders, so the weight of the two wooden pails rested on the shoulders rather than in each hand.

The six-room Winthrop home was larger than most at that time, but no mention is made of the governor's office. He probably conducted state business in the study as he had been accustomed to doing in England. By 1792, when George Washington sent William Blount to Tennessee to assume the duties of "Governor of the Territories South of the River Ohio," Blount had built a separate building directly behind his home that served as his office while negotiating with the Indians. Incidently, the Blount home was the first frame house built west of the Allegheny Mountains, and that lumber had to be brought over the mountains by oxen teams.

Judging by some of the wills left by the more prominent men in the Colonies, one gets the feeling things used around that kitchen fireplace, and later the other fireplaces, were among their most prized possessions. One man, considered quite wealthy at the time, listed his pewter candlesticks along with a pair of "great brass andirons and a pair of small andirons." He also listed a pair of "doggs" that we can only assume was a pair of plainer andirons or what was often referred to as "firedogs." A pair of tongs, fire pan, and bellows were also listed.

Key for tightening the rope beds

Victorian inkwell

In the towns and villages where the men were beginning to make money and build larger houses, furniture might be ordered from England, Germany, or even France. But the majority of the settlers, those striving to eke a living out of the land or in the process of moving farther inland, had to depend on their own ability or that of their neighbors to provide furniture.

Some of the pieces were better than others; it all depended on the skill or talent of the man making it. As time passed, the more skilled began to devote more time to furniture making and less to other chores. In some areas these men became known as "turners" because they turned out furniture, the natives said.

The Pilgrims only brought one piece of furniture with them. This was a chest filled with their worldly possessions. The chest, believed to be the first piece of furniture created, was devised during the Middle Ages to fit the needs of the nomadic, warring people who banded together for safety's sake. They often built fortresses, even castles, to try to prevent the invasion of other warring tribes. The groups grew as peasants flocked to the fortresses for protection and stayed to become a part of the group or tribe. If they lost the fight, or simply decided to move on to greener pastures, the lords, vassals, rich men, and poor would be ready to move at a minute's notice. They packed everything they owned in their chest, then loaded it on a sumpter mule for traveling.

Early etching of woman with shoulder yoke

Blacksmith-made andirons

Hessian andirons

Plain andirons, often called firedogs

19

The advantage of the chest was that it filled all the needs of the people. It was a seat, a table, a bed, and it provided storage for one's clothing, money, and chattel.

Once the pioneers acquired other pieces of furniture, the chest was not nearly as important, but it never lost its popularity entirely. In fact, its rise and decline has been recorded through the years. It made its first big comeback as a dower chest, a name that would later be changed to a hope chest. As a dower chest, it held all the linens a young girl could make. The linens were destined for her new home once she was married. The hope chest was simply a continuation of the old dower chest. Surprisingly, the old cedar chest that served as a hope chest less than half a century ago is making a comeback along the antiques trail.

The lowly safe, now known as the pie safe, is believed to have originated early in the Colonies. The Colonists were desperate for ways and means of preserving food, if only for a couple of days. Chances are the first ones were a variation of the English livery cupboard or larder cupboard. The livery cupboard could be either a hanging or a standing cupboard, with ventilated front made of wicker or slats, crisscrossed to make an openwork front. It was small, as it was used beside the bed to hold food and drink in case the occupants got hungry during the night.

The Colonists were surrounded by forests filled with wild game and streams filled with fish, yet they could only catch or kill enough for a couple of days, as they had no way to keep or preserve the meat. Those daily hunting expeditions tended to create overkill; the Colonists couldn't kill half a deer no matter how much they would have liked to. They had to kill the whole deer, and eat what they could before it spoiled, or try to find a neighbor with whom they could share it. In 1650, one family in Maryland was quoted as saying they would prefer eating a crust of dry bread to eating any more venison after consuming part of eighty deer during a three-month period. This amounted to almost one deer a day.

Potatoes and apples were packed in barrels or in the ground, while beans, peppers, apples, and other fruits were dried. Butter could also be packed away.

Potatoes, easily grown and stored, rivaled bread as the staff of life. Early settlers tried any number of ways to save their potatoes from one harvest to another, and finally settled on a method that was somewhat reliable. When the potatoes were harvested, they were allowed to dry thoroughly, and then were packed in barrels. The barrels were stored in basements, cellars, or caves.

To solve part of the food storage problem then, the settlers built the humble safe from maple, pine, walnut, or cherry, depending on what kind of lumber was available at the time. Or, the safe could be built of several types of lumber scraps. If the woods didn't blend well, the builder probably painted the safe.

The old southern saying, "Too poor to paint, and too proud to whitewash" apparently only applied to the house itself, as some of that old furniture had a half dozen or more heavy coats of paint—all in different colors. Settlers were also generous with the coats of varnish they put on old furniture. Contrary to what some think, the buckling of the finish on late oak furniture doesn't make it that old; it has just had too many coats of cheap varnish.

No doubt woven willow withes, a form of loosely woven basketry, covered some of the doors of the early safes. Slats were also used to make a latticed effect, and then there were the beautifully pierced tin inserts in the doors. It is believed that tin piercing originated with the people who saved the tins from commercially packaged foods that were shipped to the western trading posts. They pierced the tin so the food would have air, and put it in the doors.

Early English oak chest

Three-door icebox

A patent for an icebox was issued in 1803, but it was well into the late 1800s before iceboxes became readily available. The delay in building iceboxes was probably due to the lack of commercially made ice. Without ice, the icebox was worthless in summer—the time when it was needed the most. The safes continued to be used and eventually were factory made. They were used well into this century, long after iceboxes and ice became available, because not everyone could afford to buy ice every few days.

Shortly after settling in the North, the settlers learned they could build an icehouse, usually on the side of a hill, and stock it with ice from the frozen ponds and lakes. It would last well into summer. Icehouses were built as far south as middle Kentucky, and some are still there today as part of the restoration of fine old homes.

Even with the icehouses—or without them—it was not unusual for a family to have several old safes. The purpose of the safe was not only to keep the food in a cool place, but to protect it from the plentiful insects and rodents. There was no screen wire even for the doors of the homes, so the safes were essential. As soon as screen wire became available, it was used in the doors of some safes, especially in the southern part of the country.

In later years, the safes became known as pie safes, as they were used more for storing pies and cakes than other foods. By this time, the housewife

Two-door icebox

had a bit more leisure time for social events, such as family picnics, quilting bees, or a "Dinner on the Grounds" at church. These affairs offered her an opportunity to show off her baking skills. In preparation, she might bake pies and cakes for a week prior to the event. The pies and cakes were stored in the safe, and the family was allowed to eat those that "didn't turn out well."

Before the advent of the icehouse, icebox, or the pie safe, the settlers were beginning to acquire a few pieces of furniture that would be used in the kitchen. One of their first acquisitions was a table and chairs. The table was used both for dining and as a work table, while the chairs were used at the table for dining and around the fire for the social hour. The first tables were made of several boards fastened together and supported on legs that resembled the later carpenter's sawhorses. They were called trestles, even when the tops were beautifully done and the crossed legs attached. The first tables were also called table-boards, and the cloths used on them called board cloths.

Those settlers were not only ingenious, but thrifty. Much of the furniture they made served more than one purpose. For instance, the hutch table was and still is both a chair (when the circular top is raised) and a table (when it is lowered). Most hutch tables were round. A similiar piece, called a table settle, was also made. Its base was a settle or bench, while the table top was oblong.

Once the settlers had acquired that first table, the wife usually wanted another—maybe to hold the wooden bucket of water and the gourd dipper for drinking. The husband might be able to build one, or he might barter a day or two of plowing with a neighbor who was a better craftsman. By whatever method, they slowly furnished the cabin.

Pie safe with long drawer across bottom

Squatty pie safe

Tall pie safe made of oak

23

Early settle

Settle back could be lowered to make a table.

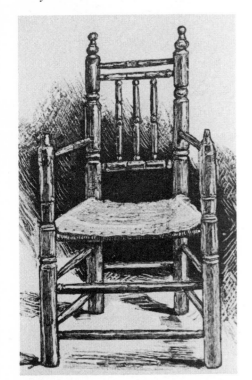

Brewster type chair

Low homemade work table

Chairs ranged from the crude to the now rare Brewster-type chair. Also made in those early years were the so-called straight chairs, with seats often made of cowhide. Rockers were also being put on the chairs to make them more comfortable. Settlers even made a two-seater that served a dual role: it fit into the wagon so that the ladies could ride in comfort to church on Sunday, and then it was put back in the kitchen for family and guests to use the rest of the week.

The writing chair had a swing-away section on the right arm that could be used for writing or for working on accounts. Some of the writing sections were stationary.

There was a time when one could say that certain pieces of furniture were made by certain craftsmen from a particular area. But as the popularity of antiques increased, so did the transfer of antiques from their old home bases. Dealers have crisscrossed the country buying antiques in one area and selling them in another. However, it is still interesting to note a few regional traits. For instance, corner cupboards are still much more popular in the East and mountain areas than in the South. It seems as though corner cupboards are preferred in the areas that were first settled, while those settled later leaned toward cabinets or cupboards that sat flat against the straight wall. Another interesting sidelight is the chair leg. Chairs known to have been made and used in the East and on into the mountains had long legs, while those found in the southern part of the country had legs that appeared to have been sawed off just below the bottom round. A tour guide in a southern restoration attributed this to the fact the chairs with long legs were easily overturned in the wagons as the settlers moved southward, so they simply sawed them off. Another guide called the short-legged chair a ''churn chair'' and said it was cut off so the housewife would have less trouble churning.

The pioneers felt the need to keep records—of their business, their slaves, their livestock, and bills they might owe. For that reason, they began building desks, some of which remained in the kitchen long after the family had a larger house. If the house were large and the family wealthy, they would probably add a secretary-bookcase in later years. But for a century or so, they slowly worked up from the crude homemade desk to the so-called plantation desk. Later they added small, plain desks and chairs for the children to use while studying, but some children continued to sit on the built-in benches on either side of the fireplace and study by the light from the fire.

High-backed, homemade rocker

Well-made kitchen work table

Chair with swing-away writing arm, often called a writing desk

Early lift-top desk

Another version of the lift-top desk

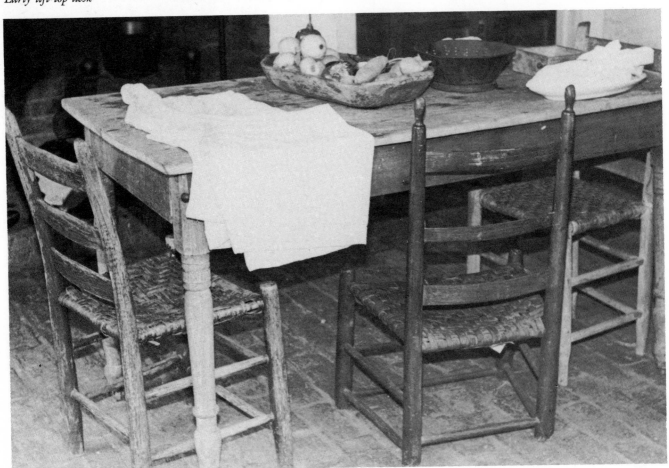

Table and chair with sawed-off legs

Early, fine-quality corner cupboard

Corner cupboard with solid doors

Not even in the homes of the more affluent did one find china and silverware in those first days. Since there were no forks, settlers had to eat with their fingers, which made napkins a necessity. No doubt most of those early napkins were little more than pieces of fabric, but later the ladies would become renowned for their snowy white tablecloths and napkins. In the latter part of the 1800s when the revival of needlework was in full swing, they made the most beautiful tablecloths and napkins covered with embroidery or drawn work and edged with fancy handmade laces.

In the beginning, settlers had to do the best they could with what they had. In this case, it was generally a trencher—a plate made from a block of wood measuring about 10″ × 12″. They usually didn't have enough trenchers for everyone. The husband and wife might share one, while several of the children would share another. They claimed it showed unity and affection and were perfectly satisfied with the arrangement. In fact, when a few skilled men with the necessary tools tried to make trenchers for each family member, the settlers considered it extravagant. Those first settlers were a frugal lot.

The wooden trenchers were so highly prized, they were mentioned in wills and inventories right along with the house, land, livestock, and the "cubberd cloth," thought to be a specially made cloth for use on the shelves of the cupboard.

Beverages such as milk and cider were served in wooden mugs or tankards with or without covers. Wooden pitchers were also available for storing and serving the beverages.

It was nearly a century before the wooden trenchers and tankards gave way to pewter. Plates or chargers were made of pewter, and by this time spoons and forks were being used. Some of the settlers moving South and West used the horns of slaughtered cattle to make various items, including drinking cups or glasses. They were also used to make horns for gunpowder and hunting horns used to call dogs out on a hunt.

Pewter chargers, plates, and tankards were definitely status symbols. They needed to be stored where they were easily reached and where they could be shown off. To accomplish this, settlers began using old English dressers, sometimes called Welsh dressers or New England dressers, and later called hutches.

Pewter plate

Homemade version of the plantation desk

28

The style of the dressers might vary some, but basically they had legs almost as high as a table's, two to four drawers across the front, and a row of shallow shelves across the top. They generally stood against one wall of the kitchen holding rows of pewter and maybe a few pieces of earthenware.

The people from each country brought with them the customs and ways of the old country, so not everybody used the dressers. The Dutch preferred the plate rack, spoon rack, and knife rack, for instance.

China was not common either in England or America during the seventeenth century. There was a little Delftware coming out of Holland, but it was in limited supply. Shortly thereafter, china and "purselin" began to filter into the Colonies. About this time, wealthier people began to build large homes. The big ship owners made lots of money transporting the harvest from the Colonies back to England, then returning with a paying load of supplies. And the merchants and planters also became affluent. They could now afford many of the luxuries, and they began to indulge themselves.

At first the settlers had indentured servants from their native countries, but then they bought slaves, some of whom worked in the kitchen. Though there were some improvements, most kitchens were basically the same. They were, however, still the center of much activity. The mistress might have moved to the parlor, but she returned to the kitchen regularly to supervise the work.

Early oak Welsh dresser

Homemade hutch

There was still a tremendous amount of heat in the kitchen. The fires burned a good part of the time, from before daylight until about dark. As the larger houses were built, the kitchens were built away from the main house, connected by a covered walkway or porch so the servants could carry the food hot from the kitchen right to the table in the dining room. This was a far cry from the way meals were served in the log cabins.

As china replaced pewter, the corner cupboard began to replace the dressers. Part of the corner cupboard's appeal was its storage space. It offered a great deal of storage, yet took up little space in the room. It was exactly what the name implied—a cupboard for the corner—and as such it fit into any corner of the room, thereby utilizing otherwise wasted space. Some corner cupboards were made with solid wooden doors, while others had glass panels. Some were made by well-known makers, while others were made by men trying to furnish their own homes.

The cupboards were made of maple, pine, cherry, and walnut, or maybe a combination of woods. The man on the prairie might have seen one in the home of the local banker, then gone home to try to copy it, using whatever

Handmade pewter spoons on spoon rack

Later pine dresser or hutch

materials were available. In his wildest imagination, he could never have dreamed that collectors today would be willing to pay such prices for the cupboard he put together in the barn.

Fifty years ago it was almost impossible to find a home in the mountains, no matter how lowly, that didn't have a gorgeous corner cupboard in the kitchen. It was usually made of walnut, cherry, or a combination of those two woods. As people acquired the more modern kitchen cabinet, they discarded the old corner cupboards. Some were left outside to rot, while others were bought by observant travelers in the areas—sometimes for as little as $3 to $5 each.

More than once the question has been asked, "How did our ancestors keep so much of their beautiful china intact?" The answer is simple: "They didn't use it." They may have used it for social affairs, but those affairs were infrequent. The china was kept in cabinets where it could be seen, on dressers, in presses, on mantels, and on specially built plate and cup rails and racks.

Sugar was so expensive and hard to get that only the rich ever had enough to store away. To protect it, they built sugar chests with sturdy locks. The mistress of the house carried the key and supervised the rationing of the sugar to the kitchen. Sugar chests weren't plentiful then, so they are rare and quite expensive today.

Low corner cupboard with glass doors

Cherry sugar chest

Homemade walnut corner cupboard

China platters were popular for use on hutches

There were never locks and keys on the meal chests—the various types of chests built to store meal after the corn was ground. Corn was plentiful, and as soon as there were commercial water-powered mills, the meal was plentiful, too. Some of the meal chests, especially those with the lift top and false drawers, are highly desirable!

The by-products of the corn, the cob and the shuck, were also utilized. The shucks were used to make a type of mop used for scrubbing floors. Holes were drilled in a thick piece of wood approximately 8″ × 15″, and the shucks were twisted tightly into each hole. When a handle was attached, the housewife had a "scrub broom." It worked well with lye soap on the wide pine boards that formed the floors in the early homes. When the shucks wore out, they were replaced with new ones.

Pioneer women loved beauty, but had little of it in their lives. They sought beauty and color wherever they could find it. It was difficult to find a cabin as late as this century that didn't have an abundance of colorful flowers blooming by the picket fence that surrounded the yard. In winter the ladies made corn-shuck flowers dyed with the same dye used for wool. This craft has been revived in recent years, and now the corn-shuck flowers can be found at restorations and arts and crafts shows.

For lack of money to buy the beautiful dolls imported from France and Germany, the poor pioneer women made dolls of corn shucks and corncobs for their children. This craft is also being revived, as the older people remember the fun they had with those dolls. There was such a fascination for these dolls that mothers continued to make them for their children well into this century. It is difficult to find the old corn-shuck and corncob dolls, but the new ones are available at prices ranging from around $5 to $8 for the corn shuck, to $10 or $12 for the corncob dolls. The latter are more expensive because they require dresses and bonnets that have to be made by hand.

Corn shucks were also used for seats in homemade chairs, but I've found no one so far who can explain the process. Apparently the shucks were worked or twisted into rope and then used like oak splints.

Corn-shuck flowers

Small lift-top meal chest with false drawer front

Tall meal chest

33

Foundation for corncob doll

Bare-headed corncob doll

Corn-shuck doll

Not all the chests designated as meal chests were used for storing corn-meal. Some were used to store flour ground from wheat. Later, in some areas of the South, barrels were more popular than the chests for storing meal and flour.

Another rare piece that is avidly sought by collectors today is the hunt board. The food and beverages prepared in the kitchen were often placed on the hunt boards in the mornings so a plantation owner and his guests could serve themselves after returning from a Virginia-type hunt or exhilarating horse-back ride. This was probably the beginning of the buffet meal. Since the hunt boards were handmade, they vary in size, style, and material used.

Wooden dough boxes and dough trays used in bread and biscuit mak-ing are also in demand today. The trays are excellent for displaying an arrange-ment of fall leaves, berries, fruits, or vegetables. Many of the dough boxes have had legs attached and now repose in living rooms, dens, or playrooms, where they serve as a table and offer storage space under the lift top for maga-zines or needlework.

Because sugar was expensive and hard to come by, most foods were sweetened with honey. Earlier the housewife would make a little jelly and jam for the family, always sweetening it with honey. As time passed and sugar became more plentiful and less expensive, she began to make enough jellies and jams to last all winter. This posed a problem of storage. It was soon solved by small jelly cupboards.

Like the early pie safe, the jelly cupboard was homemade and could, therefore, be any size or shape and made of any type of wood. Some were excellent examples of the cabinetmaker's art, while others were crude. Their doors were of screen wire, or pierced tin. In recent years, some have been seen with glass panels, which may have been added later to turn the jelly cupboard into a small display piece.

Dough box with legs attached

34

Hip bathtub

Jelly cupboard with screen wire in door

Glass replaced early material in doors and sides

Pine homemade kitchen cabinet

Well-built pine kitchen cabinet

If the first settlers could have returned to the area during the last quarter of the nineteenth century, they wouldn't have believed their eyes. There were actually bathrooms in some of the larger farm homes. The late Cassius Clay of Kentucky built a tank or reservoir on the roof of his house to catch and hold rain water for use in the leaded tin bathtub and to flush the homemade commode.

By this time, cleanliness had become next to godliness, and everything from clothing to household linens had to be sparkling white. Those without the new-fangled bathrooms used a tin washtub placed in the kitchen and filled with hot water from the stove. In summer they might take the tubs out near the well for their baths, or they might go down to the creek. In the cities, people bought the commercially made bathtubs that were similiar to the tin washtubs except for their tall, reclining backs. In the catalogues they were called Hip bathtubs. An elongated tub described as having a wood bottom, a green japanned outside, pink inside, with heavy wire end handles, and measuring six feet long was described as a Plunge bathtub. The handles were used to move it from the kitchen or bedroom back to wherever it was stored during the week.

Woodburning stoves became popular in the kitchen, beginning with the plain Franklin stove and growing to the big kitchen ranges with ovens, a hot-water reservoir on the side, and a "warming closet" on top. No longer did the housewife want the old black iron stoves that had to be polished every week. She wanted a new enameled or granite ware stove in a bright color to make her kitchen bright and cheerful and cut down on the cleaning.

Kitchen cabinets were also becoming popular. Finally the housewife had a place to put her pots and pans, as well as a small work space.

The later commercially built cupboard had a counter top and a built-in meal and flour storage bin that enabled a housewife to keep working without so many trips to the flour and meal barrels. Most cupboards also had a pull-out dough board. There was storage space in the top for mixing bowls and everyday dishes, while the bottom furnished more storage space. It was a dream come true for the housewife who had been struggling with fireplace cooking or the small woodburning cook stoves. In some of the later, factory-built models, the flour bin or container had its own sifter. This eliminated the need for the old, round, wire screen sifters.

In recent years, this type of kitchen cabinet has experienced unprecedented popularity. Some of this can be attributed to the variety of styles available. But since the cupboards are so popular with young couples, nostalgia could be part of the appeal.

Housewives struggled through all kinds of adverse conditions trying to save as much of the family food supply as possible. They used granite ware milk cans to lower milk into the well, where it would stay cool and unspoiled. And they learned how to can excess food for winter. Then the icebox was introduced. It was not the answer to all their problems, but it did keep the food fresh for several days. With commercially made ice came icemen who traveled the streets on horse-drawn wagons and, later, trucks to deliver ice. Along with the iceboxes, other collectibles were created—ice picks, now more valuable if they bear an advertiser's name, and ice tongs that are now used to hold modern paper towels in "country" kitchens.

There are many other antiques and collectibles associated with the kitchen such as iron pots and pans, the copper cooking utensils, tools used for various cooking chores, iron kettles used to heat water for baths as well as tea, and many cooking tools that were handmade for a specific, now outdated chore.

There are other antiques associated with the early rural homes or cabins. Cattle, horses, and sheep might have been allowed to roam over the countryside in those early days, but there was always a fence around the house to protect the housewife's vegetable garden and her flowers. In some areas, the fence might have been made of rocks or pickets, but the most popular in all areas was the rail fence. Today the old rail fences are reassembled around modern homes for a nostalgic appearance.

Rugs or carpeting in kitchens is definitely new. The first cabins had dirt floors, but as soon as settlers had the time and materials, they began laying wooden floors made of pine boards 18″ to 24″ wide. These served well for many years. During this time, settlers acquired rugs or, as they called them, "carpitts." The more affluent bought oriental carpets, while others made hooked and woven rugs or stenciled floor cloths. There does seem to have been some confusion with the use of the word "rug," as there were table rugs as well as bed rugs mentioned in old wills and inventories. Apparently they were first used for warmth on the beds and in later years were used on the floors.

Late factory-built kitchen cabinet

Pine homemade kitchen cabinet

Corner of stenciled floor cloth. This old craft is being revived

Granite ware wood-burning cook stove

Rail fences were used around the larger homes

No records have been found of rugs being used on kitchen floors. A century or so ago, a housewife might have used the rags from worn clothing to make a braided rug, or even have woven one on her loom. She might then have put it in the kitchen where she most often stood so it would "cushion" her feet.

Honeymoons were unheard of until recent years. In the old days, once a couple was betrothed, the young man began building a home. The bride brought to the home her dower or hope chest, with gorgeous household linens, quilts, and coverlets—everything she would need in her new home. Once the ceremony was over, the couple simply went to their new home to start building their lives together. But in some areas, there was another celebration—the charivari. A group of the newlyweds' friends and neighbors would gather around midnight, then march around the couple's house beating on pots, pans, or anything noisy. The ingenious ones devised the loudest noisemaker of all, the rattletrap.

It has been said that similiar contraptions were used by the early settlers to warn of impending Indian attacks, and during the Civil War to alert sailors of approaching enemy ships. In different parts of the country, the noisemakers probably differed in style and shape, but they all had one thing in common—they could produce ear-splitting noises.

Hickory rattletrap or noisemaker for use at charivaris

Elaborate factory-built oak kitchen cabinet

Illustration of old kitchen

Old etching of kitchen

Copper teapots often sat on the hearth

Old fireplace restored

Early stove

Cooking was moved from the fireplace to the stove

Iron teakettle with granite ware exterior

Pewter coffee pots

Later baby beds replaced the cradles

Piggins

Children's toys were kept in the kitchen

Stoneware pitchers were part of the kitchen utensils

43

Table

Kitchen whet rock for sharpening knives   *Higher quality*

Round table with matching chairs

Early butterfly table

Small, round drop-leaf table

Early bench on side of table

Walnut table with casters; cradle on top

Different type of drop-leaf table

Pair of homemade children's chairs without seats

Homemade rocker in the comb-back Windsor style

Straight chair after the Shaker style

Child's highchair

47

Fireside bench with cane-bottomed chair

Rocker made in the Shaker style

Electrified hanging lamps are still used in the kitchen

Southern country dry sink

Dipping candles

Single angle lamps were often used in the kitchen

An iron boot scraper could always be found on the steps outside the kitchen door

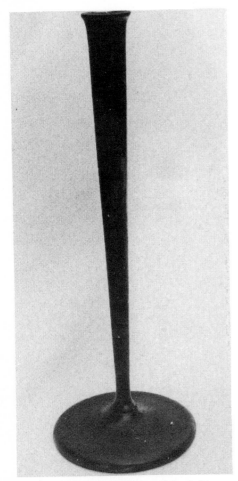

Wooden lathe-turned vases might hold a single blossom on the kitchen table, circa 1900.

Late cupboard with herbs drying and flour barrel in corner

Baskets on chest showing their original uses

All types of baskets were used in the kitchen

Kegs first held cider, then vinegar, in the kitchen

Kitchen table with open-top corner cupboard in background

Later lathe-turned wooden compotes could be found in the kitchen

Homemade ash-hopper with crock pot set to catch the lye

2
Wash on Monday

Ever since Eve, the female of the species has been responsible for the home. She somehow also fell heir to all the chores connected with the home, including the gathering, preparing, and preserving of the foods, as well as making, mending, and keeping clean all the clothing worn by the family.

It all began in America on that eventful Monday in 1620 when the Pilgrims landed in the New World and went ashore to wash the dirty clothing that had accumulated during the trip. This was the first chore performed in America, and it seemed to set a precedent. The settlers continued to wash on Monday, the first workday of the week.

Those first settlers didn't have enough clothing to make it necessary for them to wash weekly, and they weren't really that concerned about having freshly laundered clothes every day. The men wore the same leather pants and shirts all winter—and sometimes all summer as well. Old-timers say that as late as the turn of the present century, children of most rural families only had two new outfits each fall for school. City children might have had more, depending on the whims and income of the family. But in the rural areas where the children only attended school for four or five months each year, parents felt two outfits were ample. Children took off their "school clothes" as soon as they got home each day, then hung them up "to air" so they could be worn again the following day. The clothes they had worn the previous year or had been passed down by an older sister or brother were considered good enough to wear while "doing their night-work," which consisted of drawing water from the well to fill all the buckets and the reservoir on the stove, bring in enough wood to fill the wood box behind the stove and the box near the fireplace in winter, feed some of the farm animals, and help with any other chores where needed.

America was a new world with a new beginning, and for many it was only natural that new customs and new rules had to be established. Many would follow the customs and habits of their native countries, but since they were seeking freedom, mostly for religious beliefs, they must have felt the need to establish new customs that would be in keeping with their beliefs and new surroundings.

During the first century, they probably did what had to be done on a first come, first served basis. After all, life was unbelievably harsh for those early settlers, what with the hard winters, living in caves, and scrambling for food just to stay alive. They didn't have much time to be concerned about doing things on schedule—they were too concerned about survival.

But as more people arrived and they became a bit more secure, there was time for organization. Then, as now, there were probably women who complained that they were unable to get all their chores done, while others had no problems at all. Therefore it was only natural that someone would work out a schedule for housework. Many housewives soon began doing the chores by the schedule.

The first, or older version, of housekeeping rules was to wash on Monday, iron on Tuesday, bake on Wednesday, brew on Thursday, churn on Friday, mend on Saturday, and go to church on Sunday.

Iron wash pot painted white and used as a planter

Wash pot with blacksmith-built stand

A later version moved baking to Saturday, while Wednesday became the day for mending or sewing. Brew or brewing is interpreted to mean that one day was set aside to make apple cider. The first settlers had been warned not to drink the water, and had therefore substituted cider as their primary beverage. When the water controversy was cleared up and it was no longer necessary to make cider on a weekly basis, Thursday was designated as marketing day. People were no longer growing everything they ate; instead, they were going to the markets to buy from the growers or merchants who specialized in one particular food.

Just as the first settlers had adjusted to the various problems as they arose, their descendents continued to adjust to whatever changes took place. There were few, if any, jobs for women outside the home, so their entire life revolved around caring for their families and their home. There was nothing else to occupy their time, so they worked at these chores with a vengeance. To maintain their schedules and have a home clean enough to impress their friends, they often added, deleted, and reversed the schedule of homemaking chores.

As the towns and villages grew into small cities, it was no longer feasible to keep cows on the commons. Farmers then assumed the task of supplying the "town folk" with dairy products. They began adding a few cows to their herd so they could sell milk, butter, and cheese.

This relieved the city dwellers of churning and making cheeses on Friday, and they began using this day for housecleaning. As the size of the homes increased, more time was required to keep them clean.

The rules first established for Monday, Tuesday, and Sunday have never changed. It is doubtful that the ladies who scheduled these chores knew or cared that the Pilgrims washed on Monday. It probably just seemed a good idea to start the week off by washing all the dirty clothes and household linens. Then there were the dirty tablecloths and napkins from Sunday dinner, which may have included the married children, their families, and other guests, including the minister and his family. It was not unusual for twenty-five to thirty people to eat at one home on Sunday. This created a pile of laundry for Monday morning. Whatever the reason for the decision to wash on Monday, a precedent was set.

In those early days, especially in the mountains, recipes or rules were never written or recorded. Instead, they were passed by word of mouth from mother to daughter for generations. Therefore, it was surprising to find a note an unknown mother penned to her daughter describing the best way to do the family laundry. This note could very well have been put in the wash pot the mother was giving her daughter as a wedding present. She wrote:

1. Build a fire in the backyard to heat kettle of rainwater.
2. Set tubs so smoke will not blow in your eyes if wind is present.
3. Shave a whole cake of lye soap in the boiling water.
4. Sort clothes in three piles—one of white clothes, one of colored, and one of rags and britches.
5. Stir flour in cold water until smooth, then thin down with boiling water to make starch.
6. Rub dirty spots on the board, then boil them. Rub colored clothes, but do not boil. Take white things out of kettle with broom handle, then rinse, blue, and starch.
7. Hang clothes on line except tea towels, which should be spread on the grass. Hang old rags on the fence.
8. Pour rinse water in flower beds.
9. Scrub privy seat and floor with soapy water.
10. Turn tubs upside down. Put on a clean dress, comb hair. Make a cup of tea to drink while you sit and rest a spell, and count your blessings.

Early scrub board

Two styles of iron wash pots

Laundry basket filled with clothes

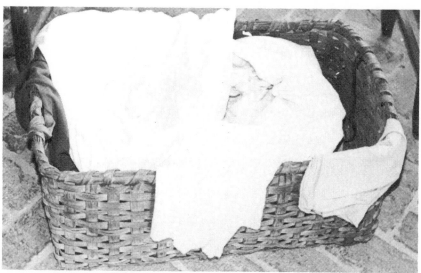

Wooden washtub on legs

These rules appear to have originated sometime between the early days when the family wash was taken to the nearby stream, and the invention of the washing machine around the turn of the twentieth century.

Compared to the modern, completely automatic washing machines, those early ones left much to be desired. They had to be manually cranked in order to agitate the laundry. Later there would be the gas models, which would agitate without assistance, if the engine didn't stop. And finally there was the washing machine as we know it today. Although the more prosperous families in the cities had washing machines, there were families in the rural areas who used the iron wash pot, washboards, and tubs until well into this century.

Some of the families considered themselves lucky if they had a hand wringer—the type that fastened on the side of the tub. By turning the handle, they could wring the water out of the clothes between rinses and before hanging on the line. Fortunate indeed were those ladies who had a washbench—a wooden slatted bench—that would accommodate two washtubs with a hand wringer in the middle.

Different style sticks used for beating the clothes as well as for dipping them out of the pot

Cut-away showing the inside of an early washing machine

Washing machine with attached wringer

56

Two styles of wooden washboards

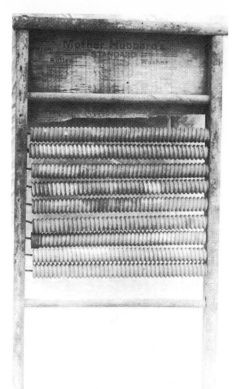

Washboard with wooden rollers

Called the Wonder Washer, this one had the handle on top

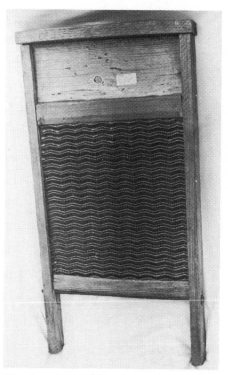

Granite ware washboard

Keeping the family clothing and household linens clean in those days was quite a chore, as housewives not only had to save rainwater or carry water from the nearest spring or stream, but also had to make the soap used to wash the clothes.

Since there were no packaged detergents in those days, the housewife had no choice except to make her own. This trend would continue for centuries, even after the majority of the people could afford commercially made soap. Housewives felt that the lye soap cleaned dirty clothes better, and they had been taught all their lives not to buy anything they could make at home.

Making lye soap was another of those time-consuming chores. In fact, it was almost a year-round chore, as housewives had to save the grease left over from both cooking and butchering, as well as the ashes from the fireplace. The grease was usually saved in barrels until time to make soap, while the ashes were put into an ash-hopper, sometimes called a leach barrel. The hopper was built on legs and the barrel placed on short stumps or bricks. Water was poured over the ashes and allowed to trickle out into a container. This was called setting the leach, or making lye.

As the ashes were added, a little more water was poured over. This continued until shortly before the housewife was ready to start making soap. As soap-making time approached, she began checking her lye. It was considered strong enough when a potato or egg would sink in it until only a portion the size of a half-dollar showed. If it wasn't strong enough to hold the potato or the egg near the top, it was run through the hopper—several times, if necessary.

Lye soap was basically the same the world over. Each housewife might have had her own little secrets for success, such as stirring with a sassafras stick. But in the end, it all boiled down to a mixture of rancid old grease and lye. Later there would be commercially made lye but as with the packaged soap, some continued to make their own.

A basic recipe for lye soap circa 1870 began as follows:

> Take a pound of lye, dissolve in three and a half gallons of boiling water, and add thereto about five pounds of grease; keep stirring and boiling until the grease and lye are completely combined which will take about five to ten hours, then add a little salt, which will separate and bring all the soap to the top. It may then be dipped out in a box which will serve as a mold, and when cold cut into bars. In boiling, it will be necessary to add water as it is boiled away. New grease will require much more than old, rancid grease. The lye remaining unused may be boiled up with the grease scraps and kettle scrapings, adding two gallons more water which will make good soft soap when allowed to cool.

Just as the type of feathers used in beds and pillows was an indication of the early housewife's abilities as a homemaker, so was the whiteness of her laundry. For that reason, she was concerned about the soap she used and took great pride in her ability to make good soap. Although women might have considered bragging a sin, they were not averse to discussing at length the "good luck" and the "bad luck" they had with their latest batch of soap.

In areas where the winters were especially harsh, it was the custom to make at least a barrel of soap in the fall—enough to last until spring. Estimates are that six bushels of ashes and about twenty-five pounds of grease were required to make one barrel of soap. It is still the custom in restorations of old homes and towns where demonstrations of the old chores are performed for people to make pots of lye soap in the fall.

Hard lye soap was considered too strong or harsh for bathing, so settlers took some of the soap while it was still soft, and tried to work it down. It was scented with "essence of sassafras" in some areas and bayberry in others. This so-called bath soap was put in tin pans, allowed to harden, then cut into bars or cakes.

There are many antiques and collectibles related to the chore of washing. Along with the wash pots or kettles that have become popular in recent years, there are the wooden tubs, buckets, many styles of washboards, graniteware, tin, brass and glass, and the antique clothes dryers. The dryers are not remotely related to the modern dryers. Instead, they look like a six- to eight-pronged rack that hung on the wall. The arms or prongs were extended when needed to hang the wet clothes on rainy days. They are quite similar to the old towel racks used in the kitchen, but have longer arms.

There also are the shoulder yokes used to bring buckets of water from the spring or creek. These have limited use today and are sought after only for their nostalgic value. They sometimes are used in country kitchens as a rack for wooden cooking tools.

Surprisingly, washing was responsible for many miniatures and toys made around the turn of the twentieth century. In those days, there were few, if any, jobs for women and girls. The only future young girls had to look forward to was getting married early and establishing a home. Since homemaking was so important, it was assumed that if the girl or girls were well trained in the art of homemaking, their chances of marriage were greater. Mothers began that training early, using miniature tools just like their own.

All-wood washboard

Wringer with large rollers

Tin washboard

Many of the toys are still available, but it is usually the adults who collect them now. In 1910, Butler Brothers advertised nearly a dozen different "laundry toys." Butler was one of the large wholesale houses at that time, and all their prices were wholesale. Occasionally, though, they would list a suggested retail price. They listed an "up-to-date set consisting of a 10″ tub with iron hoops and four turned wood screw-in legs plus a small wringer and washboard" as a good 50¢ seller. This particular model sold for $3.90 a dozen wholesale. For $8 a dozen wholesale the merchant could order a seven-piece wash set consisting of a 12″ tub, 16″ clothesline, basket, brush, washboard, and wringer. This set probably retailed for around one dollar and must have been a popular Christmas gift for little girls.

Small wooden clothespins for fastening the clothes on the line were sold in a barrel that could be used as a bank when the pins were lost or discarded. The dozen pins in the barrel sold for 5¢ retail. Small corrugated tin washboards with wooden frames sold for the same amount, while the 7″ × 15″ size sold for 10¢. Metal buckets with a grained wood finish also sold for 10¢ retail.

Toy washing machine

Toy washtub, washboard, and wringer

Sometimes small amounts of laundry were boiled on the stove

Label on dryer showing a patent date of 1887

Early clothes dryer

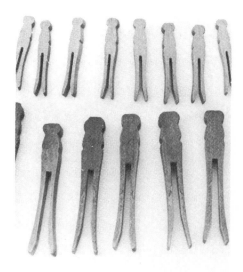

Small wooden clothespins

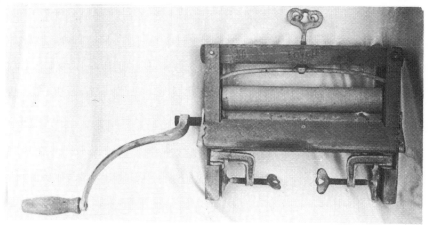

Wringer with small rollers

Assortment of irons: charcoal, sadiron, and two with detachable handles

Assortment of irons

Sadirons and charcoal iron

Gasoline irons

62

3

Iron on Tuesday

Although irons have been collected for years, little has been written about them. This is probably due to the fact that, until a decade or so ago, ironing was a hot, tiring, thankless task that had to be repeated week after week after week. Even with the electric iron, it is a chore. But nothing compares to the days when long, full dresses and even fuller petticoats, each covered with ruffles, had to be pressed with irons heated on the stove or by the fire in a fireplace. In large families with a number of popular daughters, it was not unusual to have one servant who was responsible for all the ironing.

In the southern part of the country, where the climate is hot for eight to nine months of the year, ironing was even more tiring and unbearable. In the New England states, at least, the fires were welcome most of the year.

Not only did the clothing and household linens have to be ironed, they required starching as well. With enough starch and ironing a housewife could make the cheapest cotton fabric look like expensive and desirable chintz. Around the turn of the century, mothers often put a few spoonsful of kerosene in the flour starch to give the fabric a glossy or polished finish.

It is not known exactly when the first irons were made, but there are records of their use as early as the sixteenth century. These are European records; no indications of their use in America in the early years have been found.

It is believed that the ruff, which began as a simple cotton collar with a gophered edge and became one of the most elaborate pieces of neckwear the world has ever known, is partially responsible for both starch and the iron. What began as a single, ruffled collar grew during the Elizabethan era to a dozen collars or more, all stiffly starched and perfectly pleated or ruffled.

During the sixteenth century the ruff starch was so expensive it was considered a luxury, affordable only by the affluent or nobility.

The origin of starch, like that of the iron, is unknown, but in the first century, Pliny mentioned it being made of wheat. Records from that time until the advent of the ruff are vague when it comes to starches. Along with the creation of the ruff came the introduction of starch made from potatoes. That should have made it inexpensive, but still it was described as a luxury.

When the pioneers needed starch, they first made it from potatoes, then from flour ground from wheat. With the introduction of cotton fabrics, the need for starch increased. It was only natural that someone would devise a way to make it on a large-scale basis. Two brothers, Edward and John Gilbert, built the first starch-making factory in Utica, New York, in 1807.

The big break-through in commercially made starch came when a man named Thomas Kingsford, who had been hired to manage a soap-making factory owned by William Colgate, discovered through many experiments that he could make starch from corn.

Corn was still more plentiful than wheat and less expensive. Therefore, Kingsford starch could be made at prices everyone could afford. It was an instant success, although there were still descendants of the early settlers who felt they should continue to make their own starch at home.

While the world of starch was being revolutionized, some improvements were being made in irons, too. The first ones had been hollow and were called "box irons." Hot coals were put in the box or hollow center to heat the irons. Shortly thereafter, a bar of iron was included with each iron. The iron bar was heated in the fireplace or in hot coals, then put in the box to keep the iron hot for a short time.

Old ironing boards have little use today except when painted with bright colors to brighten the kitchen

The gophering iron first appeared during the ruff period, when it was essential to smooth pleats and ruffles. Gophering irons were cylindrical, about the size of one's finger, with a long handle. No doubt the "crimping iron," and later the "pinking iron" developed from the gophering iron idea.

The box iron evolved into the sadiron, which was a solid iron bar shaped like today's irons. This iron was heated by setting it in front of the hot coals in the fireplace, and later putting it on the top of the wood-burning stove.

Years later, sadiron heaters became available. In the catalogues, they were described as being for use on "gas, gasoline, and oil stoves; heats three irons at one time." The heaters had about an $8'' \times 9''$ base, were $6\frac{1}{2}''$ high, and were made of iron, sometimes with a copper coating. They weighed around three pounds each without the sadirons and sold for about 45¢ each in 1910. Today they are selling for from one hundred fifty to two hundred times that amount.

Irons were made for every ironing chore. The average housewife might have a dozen or more irons, including the sleeve iron for long and slender sleeves. Or she might have irons of different weights for different fabrics. For instance, a small iron would be used for cotton, while the heaviest iron was used for pressing woolen garments.

A large iron, weighing approximately fifteen to twenty-five pounds, was made especially for tailors. Called a tailor's goose, it was $3''$ to $4''$ wide and about $10''$ to $12''$ long. This heavy iron was necessary for tailors who worked on woolen garments, as the extra weight was needed to press open the seams.

The Potts iron consisted of three double-pointed irons with one detachable handle. The 4-pound iron was called a polishing iron; $5\frac{1}{8}$-pound iron for general work and a $5\frac{1}{2}$-pounder were all interchangeable, fastening to the handle with a screw-type attachment directly under the round wooden handle. This set usually came with a stand, which is usually missing from antique sets today.

When the Potts irons began to appear, there were advertisements in various catalogues for pinking irons, multiple-tooth gadgets that required the housewife to insert the fabric in each recess. A later gadget identified as a pinking iron was made with five small iron rods or prongs—two pointed ones below and three above—and a scissors-like handle. The owner described it as being most useful for ironing or pleating curtains at a time when every window was covered with ruffled curtains. She said you simply heated the irons by holding them well above the fire to avoid smoke, and then slipped the pointed prongs under the ruffles and squeezed.

The most elaborate fluting irons were those made from around 1875 through 1900. In the old catalogues, they were called fluting machines, but the end results were about the same as that made by the pinking irons. The iron rods were heated in the coals, and with a pair of tongs that were part of the package deal, they were inserted into the two cogged rollers. A crank on the side rushed the ruffles through, and they came out on the other side in perfect pleats or flutes.

The charcoal iron was on the same order as the early box irons, except it took charcoal to keep it hot instead of wood coals from the fireplace.

Although a few irons were in use earlier, it is doubtful many will be found that date earlier than the nineteenth century. It seems there was a flurry of activity in the field of iron improvement beginning around 1850. One of the newest inventions at that time was a type of charcoal iron with bellows that could be inserted in a hole in the back of the iron to keep the coals burning brightly. The idea probably originated with the blacksmith's forge.

Gas irons had tanks for gasoline and air. That combination was supposed to keep the flame burning, thereby eliminating the need for a fire in the fireplace or the stove. This meant the house would be cooler, which in turn would allow the person doing the ironing to stay cooler. But all was not as well as might be expected. A few women were unable to use the irons safely; in fact, more than one spilled gas, then lighted a match before it was mopped up, causing dangerous fires.

Potts iron

Tailor's goose

Hand fluting iron

One-room log cabin

Log cabin with kitchen on back

Table with lazy susan, chairs with short legs

Fireplace with spit; pewter plates on mantel

66

Drop-leaf table used in kitchen

Pie safe

Corner cupboard

Refinished English or Welsh dresser or hutch

Cupboard with herbs hanging from the ceiling to dry

Food warmer that sat in front of the fire

Screen cover and platter on shelf above safe

Wooden washtub with attached wringer

69

Pastry roller, used to roll biscuits

Homemade honey press

Rolling pins and other wooden tools displayed over kitchen door

Patchwork quilt

Appliquéd quilt

71

Spinning wheel and early chair

Three corncob dolls

The next big step was the electric iron. The first electric iron was invented in 1889 by a man named Carpenter who lived in St. Paul, Minnesota. However, a workable electric iron was not available to the general public until 1896. Even then, there was no thermostat to control the heat. Another problem facing the electric iron manufacturers was the lack of electricity in most rural areas. It was well into the 1950s before electricity was available to the majority of farm families. They continued to use the sadiron, which probably accounts for so many being available today.

In 1900, the spirits iron was introduced. It burned methylated spirits in a tank on the front. Like the gasoline iron, it never became popular. It was better than the sadiron, but it was far from satisfactory, as there was too much danger of an explosion. Only the brave or those accustomed to working with combustible materials had much success with it.

Little use can be found for old sadirons in today's society. They make attractive additions to the hearth in dens and playrooms, and they make excellent bookends and doorstops. They also are attractive when painted white or pastel colors and decorated with decals of flowers or fruit.

Irons were reproduced as toys for children. There were toy sadirons with individual trivets. Then there was the Magic Plaiter, a wooden board with metal strips that fastened under perfectly arranged metal loops on either side. The metal strips could be arranged to make a variety of pleats. Made by Milton Bradley, it was probably actually used to pleat little girl's dresses. Now they are used for pleating doll clothes.

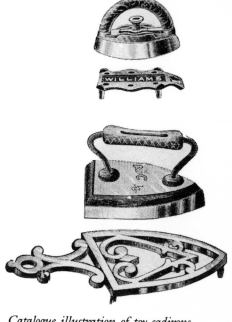

Catalogue illustration of toy sadirons

Fluting iron, also called a fluting machine

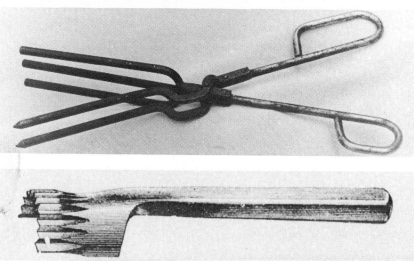

Late pinking iron

Pinking iron

73

Sadirons on heater

Fluting iron

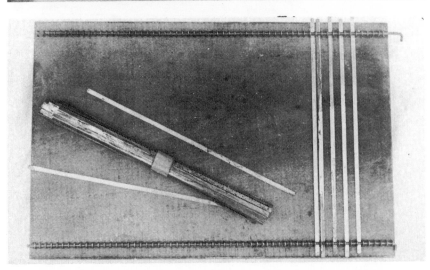

Milton Bradley's Magic Plaiter

4

Bake on Wednesday

Once our forefathers cleared the land and solved the basic problems of survival, they ate and ate heartily. Part of this could be attributed to the lack of storage methods. If a deer was killed in the morning, most of it had to be used within a couple of days before it spoiled. They lived on foods such as potatoes and corn dishes, which could be kept for longer periods of time. They did learn to dry some of the meat to make jerky, which was popular with mountain men like Sam Houston and Davy Crockett who spent days on the trail. Jerky was also popular with the settlers traveling to the West, but this was long after the Pilgrims landed.

The Indians taught settlers to live off the land. There would have been plenty of food if they had only conserved the available food as the Indians had always done. But when game was so plentiful, there didn't seem any need to save anything.

It probably never crossed the settlers' minds not to kill deer regularly, as there were literally thousands of deer when the pioneers arrived. The animals had never been harmed or even hunted, except for an occasional hunting trip by the Indians, who only killed enough to furnish food for the tribe. The deer were also killed for the skins or hides to make buckskin pants and shirts. The leather protected men's bodies as they traipsed through the woods, and it was warmer, too. Not all the leather was used in this country; much of it was shipped back to England.

The Pilgrims began their hearty eating with that first Thanksgiving or, as they called it, the Harvest Festival. "Our harvest being gotten in," Edward Winslow wrote a friend, "our governor sent four men fowling that we might after a special manner rejoice together."

Those men killed enough fowl, geese, ducks, and "a great store of wild turkeys," to last for several days, but it wasn't enough for the few Pilgrims and the ninety Indians who surprisingly accepted their invitation to come to the celebration. They probably only expected the Indians to stay one day, but they stayed for several. When the food ran out, they graciously went out and "killed five deer," and the festivities continued.

In 1631, when Governor Winthrop's family arrived from England, there was a mighty celebration. A list of the foods included "fat hogs, kids, venison, poultry, geese, and partridges." And, of course, the inevitable pumpkin pie. Other foods mentioned were vegetables "of every sort," which of necessity would be limited. Walnuts, popcorn, raisins, and citron were also mentioned, as was an abundance of cider.

The preparations for these early celebrations were probably quite mundane compared to the Thanksgivings and Christmases celebrated in the colonial homes of the important Virginia planters, such as George Washington, Thomas Jefferson, and Patrick Henry. By this time the kitchens were no longer part of the main house, but were separate buildings with a walkway to the dining room. In those kitchens, foods were still prepared in the huge fireplaces fitted with elaborate cranes, ovens, and spits or roasting jacks. Baking ovens usually were built only on one side of the fireplace, but in families that entertained often, there might be an oven on either side.

Early Staffordshire sugar dish

Wedgwood game pie tureen, circa 1825

Servants or slaves jealously guarded their positions as head of the kitchen troops. They only took orders from their mistresses and assigned kitchen chores like a top sergeant in the army.

In these homes and those of the rich city merchants and shippers, the prepared food was taken from the kitchens to the great dining rooms glowing with warm candlelight. The food was served on china with silver serving pieces. Again, these were only obtainable by the rich. Meanwhile, in the wilderness, the settlers were still looking for places to establish homes. They were still living off the land, catching fish and killing game to supplement their meager food supply.

In little over a century, things had changed so much it is doubtful the early settlers would have recognized the places or the prices. By this time most of the people in the towns and cities were buying practically everything they ate, and reports are that the quality of the beef, mutton, lamb, and poultry was excellent. Fine fish were plentiful and cheap.

By 1740, some butchers in Boston were selling beef, mutton, lamb, and veal for as much as two-pence a pound sterling, while others were selling the same meats for as little as six-pence per pound in New England money, which was little more than one penny sterling. The country had not settled on a standard monetary system. Therefore, many kinds of money were in circulation, making it difficult to translate those prices so they can be compared with today's. At that time, New England money was paper money.

Now and then, records can be found that shed a bit more light on those early food prices. In some areas, winter meat prices rose to a shilling or sixteen and two-thirds cents a pound, and sometimes went as high as fourteen-pence or twenty cents a pound.

About this same time, an English visitor writing to his family compared food prices in the Colonies with those in England. He said a turkey would cost six to seven times as much in England as it would in Boston, where the price was two shillings sterling. A fine goose that would cost as much as three shillings six-pence or four shillings in London could be bought for ten-pence in Boston.

He also mentioned a type of wild pigeon that was eaten in the Colonies and described it as larger, finer, and cheaper than those found in London.

All along the East Coast, seafoods were plentiful and cheap. Cod fish was described as "weighing a dozen pounds or more when just taken from the sea." While still alive, they sold for about two-pence sterling. Salmon weighing as much as fourteen to twenty pounds were selling for a shilling each.

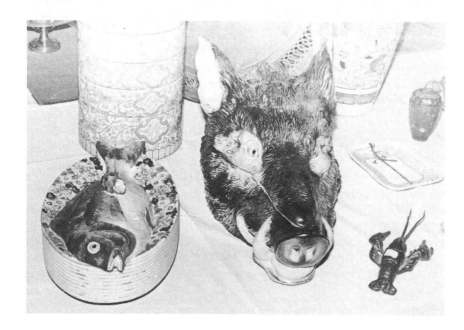

Later game dishes

There was no law against selling wild game in those days. Venison was sold "by the haunch," which probably helped to eliminate some of the random killing. Bread was sold by the loaf, but at half the price London visitors expected to pay. However, they described it as inferior to the bread at home. Cider was three shillings a barrel. Wood for heating or burning in the fireplace was considered expensive in the cities. It was still free for the cutting in the outlying areas and in the wilderness.

Even in the early days, Americans were involved in studies of various kinds. In 1750 a study was done on the "Commerce of the Colonies." It showed that "the wealth of some families, particularly persons in mercantile life, is very large." For that reason they could and did live well, as did the planters.

In fact, the menus from the plantation parties are mouthwatering. Unlike the earlier settlers, who started their meals with dessert (if hasty pudding could be called dessert), they began the meal with something like beef soup, which was made by putting twenty pounds of coarse or tough beef in eight gallons of cold water and boiling it for at least ten hours. At the end of the cooking time, the grease was skimmed off, and onions, celery, turnips, finely cut red pepper, cloves, mace, black pepper, thyme, and marjoram were added. It was then boiled until there was only four gallons of liquid or soup. The next step was to strain it through three or four thicknesses of flannel. It was then allowed to cool, and when it was cold, it became a fine jelly. Before it was served, it was heated and put in a large tureen.

There was always a turkey roasting to a turn on the spit or roasting jack in front of the roaring kitchen fire. A ham might be boiled in the ham boiler or baked in the oven, while venison, duck, fish, or oysters caught fresh that morning were being prepared. There was a variety of vegetables, along with five or six different kinds of bread, including "beaten biscuits." Then there were fancy desserts served with wines and liqueurs.

Beaten biscuits were supposed to be "as white as the driven snow when broken open," according to our ancestors. They long have been a favorite. Since methods of measuring ingredients in those days went by-guess and by-gosh, each housewife worked out a system of measuring that was right for her.

Several recipes for beaten biscuits are available, but this one from the early 1800s seems to be the best. "Put two pints of flour, one tablespoon of lard, and one teaspoon of salt into a bowl, then slowly add a half pint of half sweet milk and half water. Knead the flour mixture, stopping as soon as the flour holds together. The dough should be stiff. Beat for thirty minutes with an axe kept especially for that purpose. Or run it back and forth through a kneading trough," a homemade gadget also called a pastry roller. One old-timer mentioned "rolling out" biscuits on the pastry roller. It is quite possible the pastry roller was a copy of the earlier kneading trough. It is also possible the kneading trough was an earlier example of the dough tray. It is difficult to pin these terms down when all the pieces were handmade, designed and made to fit the needs of the person who would use them.

Biscuits continued to be a favorite, but the time needed to make them was shortened from the thirty-minute beaten biscuit method to the five-minute kneading method, used with the wooden dough trays. Cooking time remained the same, as they could be baked to a golden brown in ten to fifteen minutes when put in a covered Dutch oven or spider that was placed on a mound of red hot coals on the hearth. Today canned biscuits have relegated both the kneading trough and the dough tray to antique status.

One of the favorite desserts of those days was "tipsy-cake" served with syllabub. It would be almost impossible now to follow those recipes without lots of experimentation, as the tipsy-cake was made by baking a sponge cake, using the same amount of sugar as the weight of a dozen eggs. Half that amount of flour was used. Each cook worked out her weights and measures so that most of her baking was perfect.

Pastry roller, which could have been used earlier for beaten biscuits

The cake was cut horizontally through the center and filled with blanched almonds and jelly, then "saturated" with wine. It then was placed in a deep dish, where it was covered with a gallon of custard made by using five eggs to each quart of milk and a pound of sugar to the gallon. It was flavored with lemon and topped with syllabub. Calories were not mentioned, nor were they important in those days.

An 1865 recipe for syllabub directed the cook to: "Put into a large bowl half a pound of sugar broken small, and pour on it the strained juice of a couple of fresh lemons; stir these well together, and add to them a pint of port wine, a pint of sherry, and half a pint of brandy; grate in a fine nutmeg, place the bowl under the cow, and milk it full." Experiments have shown that about two quarts of milk is the correct amount for most taste.

This was the food enjoyed by the very affluent, those who had come from rich families in England, and who had become wealthy in America. They were enjoying the good life in the Colonies. Meanwhile at the other end of the spectrum were the settlers, who had arrived with little more than the clothes on their backs and were still struggling to eke out a living in the New World.

Tureen for serving beef soup

Wooden dough tray

Many of these still used the wooden trenchers or pewter chargers and plates, probably given to them by the rich families when they no longer wanted or needed them. They all continued to cook on fireplaces, but in the log cabins in the mountains and the farmhouses across the South and Midwest, the cooking tools and utensils were much more primitive.

Corn was actually the staff of life for the early settlers. They quickly learned how to grow corn after Powhatan, father of Pocahontas, sent some of his men to show them how to plant and grow it. He knew they would starve without sufficient food, and corn had always been the mainstay of the Indian diet.

One of the first methods of preparing corn was a preparation called "Nocake" or "Nookick," made by parching the corn in hot ashes, then beating it into a powder. The Indians carried this mixture in a leather bag on their backs so they could take out a few spoonsful and mix it with water when they were hungry.

Samp, sometimes called nawsamp, was another corn dish made by grinding unparched corn into meal and boiling it. It could be served hot or cold with milk and butter, and was described as a nourishing meal.

Indian pudding, later called Hasty Pudding after the dish made with wheat or oats and milk, was eaten by many early families on a daily basis. Since cornmeal was plentiful most of the time, this mixture of meal and milk slightly sweetened with honey was a perfect dish, as it could be put over the fire in the morning and would be ready to eat at noon. Leftovers could be kept warm and served in the evening.

Before the cornmeal was ready for cooking, there was a long process of growing and grinding. There were only a couple of years during those early times when there wasn't enough corn to furnish food for all the settlers. In those years of exception, the settlers were busy planting the lucrative new crop tobacco and didn't want to take time out to hunt for fresh game. Therefore, they gave some firearms to the Indians to do the hunting for them. Some of the Indians decided to hunt settlers as well as game, so the farmers were afraid to plant corn for a year or so, as it made an excellent cover for renegade Indians before they stormed a cabin. Corn became so scarce during that time it was selling for the equivalent of $30 to $40 a bushel.

Not everyone who came to live in the New World liked or would even attempt to eat the corn dishes. Among those were the French who settled in Louisiana. They had been accustomed to food that was less coarse, and actually detested corn. In fact, it was said the ladies organized a "petticoat rebellion" against its daily use and accused French officials of luring them to a land of milk and honey when there was little except corn dishes.

From the earliest days, the people depended on corn dishes for their very survival. And preparing those corn dishes wasn't exactly a picnic, as it was a long and time-consuming chore. After the corn was grown and harvested, it had to be ground into meal, as most of the corn dishes were either baked or boiled. For this chore, settlers used portions of logs hollowed out to form a sort of mortar, while a mallet of sorts was used as a pestle. This tool was copied from one used by the Indians.

Corn, wheat, and oats not only kept the pioneers from starvation, they were also responsible for some of the choice antiques we collect today. Beginning with the frails that were used to separate the wheat grains from the stalks, the list includes sieves for sifting the meals and flour to separate them from particles of husk, dough boxes and trays, the later commercially made bread risers and bread makers, bread knives, biscuit cutters, rolling pins, dough and pastry rollers, and a large assortment of iron baking pans. Of more interest, probably because they are less plentiful, are the cooking tools, such as the old waffle irons and the desirable wafer irons.

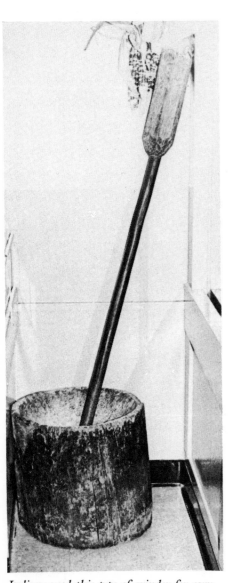

Indians used this type of grinder for corn

Long-handled waffle irons for cooking over
an open fire

Early iron pot for fireplace cooking

Pioneers seemed to prefer this type of
grinder

Assortment of utensils for fireplace cooking

Old illustration showing various ways to grind corn

Corn drier

Tin bread raiser, often called a bread riser

Later gray granite ware bread raiser with tin lid

Bread maker or mixer, circa 1914

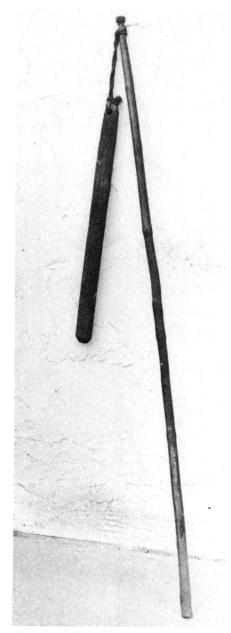

Homemade frail for threshing wheat

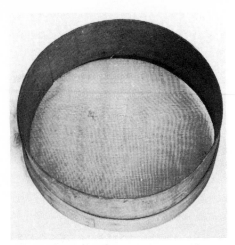

Wooden bound screen wire sieve or sifter

Sifter with coarse wire

Wafer or wafering irons were made into the last quarter of the 1800s because there were still those who cooked on the fireplace. If they were fortunate enough to have one of the newfangled woodburning cookstoves, they simply removed an eye so the wafer iron could be placed directly over the open fire. Although tipsy-cake was still served in the homes of the rich, the poor were delighted to have wafers made by this recipe:

> Add one cup sweet butter to one cup sugar. Mix until creamy. Add two well beaten eggs, one teaspoon powdered cinnamon and enough flour to make a batter that can be formed into small balls the size of large marbles. Place the balls on a hot, buttered wafer iron, close the iron and hold it for a few minutes in or directly over the fire—just long enough to brown the wafer delicately. They are very tasty if curled carefully over a round stick when hot.

This was one of the easy recipes. Like the beaten biscuits, the preparation of most foods in those early days was long and time-consuming. Perhaps that is the reason that one day, Wednesday, was set aside for baking. Once housewives had acquired ovens built in the side of the fireplace, they probably spent all day Wednesday just baking. Baking bread for a big family could have taken most of the day. While they were working on the breads, they might as well bake a cake or some cookies. They usually had all the ingredients, as most families kept a few chickens for eating and for eggs and a few hives of bees for honey, much of which was used for sweetening. For years it was considered the proof of a good housewife if she baked on Wednesday.

Everything in those early days was time-consuming. With our automatic coffee makers it is hard to realize that our ancestors had to parch the coffee beans, grind them into a coarse meal in the coffee mill, then boil the meal in water to make coffee.

One of the ways to make delicious coffee, they said, was to boil one measure of ground coffee in three measures of water. The pot in which the coffee was to be prepared was placed on "hot ashes mixed with coals" and boiled until the coffee settled to the bottom. The coffee was then poured several times through folded flannel fabric before it was served. Later there would be strainers for removing the coffee grains from the liquid. These same strainers were also used to strain the leaves out of the tea.

The antiques and collectibles associated with cooking and baking would make a long list indeed, as they range all the way from the early iron pots and pans, trivets or gridiron, spits and roasting jacks, to the tin cookie cutters—both the handmade ones made by the traveling tinsmith, to the later commercially made ones. There were also cranberry scoops, nut crackers, and so many more.

Cabbage was easily and quickly grown, but like the potatoes and apples had to be stored. This meant burying them in a hole in the ground or making them into kraut. This in turn necessitated tools, such as the kraut cutter and later the slaw cutter. The slaw cutters are still used in a few homes today, but the kraut cutter's usefulness, like that of so many other early tools and utensils, is passé. These cutters can still be used attractively in decoration at various times of the year. They are especially attractive in the fall when filled with brilliantly colored autumn leaves and berries or colorful fruits, and again during the Christmas holidays they can be filled with fruits or decorated Christmas balls.

One of the most important tools in the early kitchens was the mortar and pestle. It was used for grinding everything from the herbs and spices used in food to the herbs and roots used in medication. Mortars and pestles were so necessary in preparing medication, they were used for years to identify the apothecary or pharmacy.

The mortar is a container or vessel made of any material from wood to iron, and it is made in a cup shape so the ingredients can be pounded to a powder with the pestle.

Early wafer irons

Iron pan for eleven muffins

Muffin pans for half dozen

Large families required muffins by the dozens

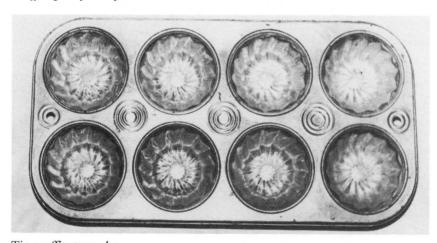

Tin muffin pans, late

Iron baking pan for Vienna rolls

Wall-hanging coffee mill

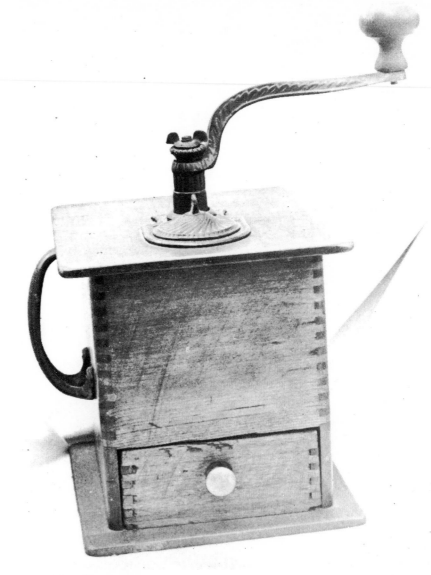

Lap coffee mill

Top of coffee mill showing how beans were placed

Container that could be fastened on grate to heat water or coffee

Cranberry scoop

Hatchet-shaped tin cookie cutter

Two heart-shaped tin cookie cutters

Cookie cutter in shape of woman's shoe

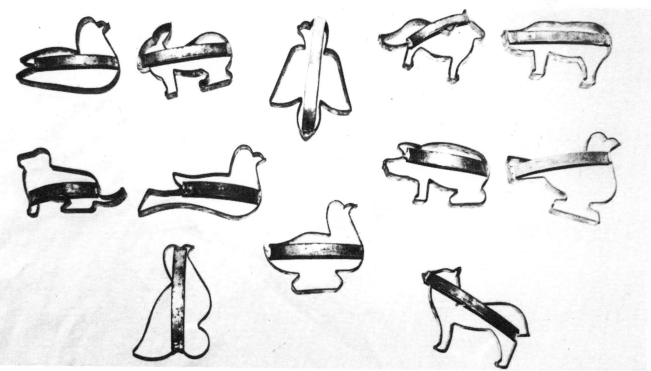

Late tin cookie cutters in animal and bird shapes

Medium-sized kraut cutter

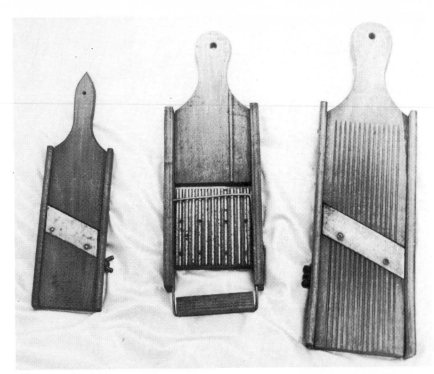

Three hand-held slaw cutters

Late ornate brass mortar and pestle

Stone mortar with wooden-handled pestle, circa 1850

Wood mortar and pestle

Plain iron mortar and pestle

Iron blacksmith-made mortar and pestle

Brass mortar and pestle

In the early days in this country, there were no doctors. When they did start practicing, they were few in number for many years. They usually settled in the towns and cities, which meant the people in the small towns and rural areas had to travel ten to twenty miles or more on horseback to get the doctor or take the sick person in the wagon. Sometimes when the illness was complicated, the settlers did go for the doctor or take the patient to him, but most of the pioneers learned to care for their own. They learned which herbs and roots could be used to cure various ailments, and they made their own medications by grinding and mixing those ingredients in the mortar and pestle. Later, doctors were more plentiful and began to settle in the small towns, but the suspicious mountain people preferred their own medication to "doctor medicine" any day.

The history of the mortar and pestle goes back to the Middle Ages, when they were an important part of any new household. It was the custom for many years for parents to give their daughters a mortar and pestle as a wedding gift.

Along with grinding herbs and spice, the mortar and pestle have been used through the years for grinding coffee beans, crushing salt, grinding pieces of loaf sugar to make fine or granulated type sugar, and crushing tobacco into snuff.

Mortars and pestles were made of iron, brass, assorted metals, and wood. The woods most often used were oak, elm, beech, walnut, and lignum vitae, the hardest wood of them all.

Tin, pewter, and earthenware molds of all kinds—those used for candies, ice creams, jellies, and puddings—are collectible today, as are the handled ware, the wooden spoons and forks, used to mix the ingredients put into the molds. There were also nutcrackers and lemon squeezers. The first were made entirely of wood, but later commercially made wooden ones were available along with metal ones.

Scales were vitally important, as so many ingredients used in cooking were weighed rather than simply thrown in the pot. The small scales had many uses, but none was more important than the weighing of farm produce, butter, cheese, and chickens, when the housewife began to have extra that could be sold to bring in much needed money.

Wooden lemon squeezer

Wooden nutcracker

Tin jelly or pudding molds

Metal nutcracker

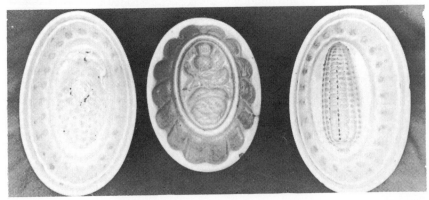

Stoneware jelly or pudding molds

90

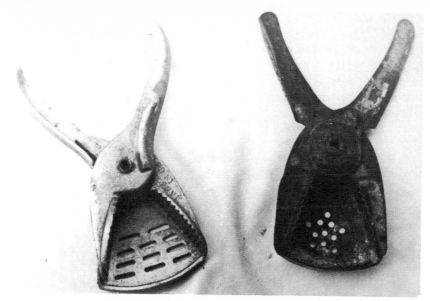

Late lime squeezers

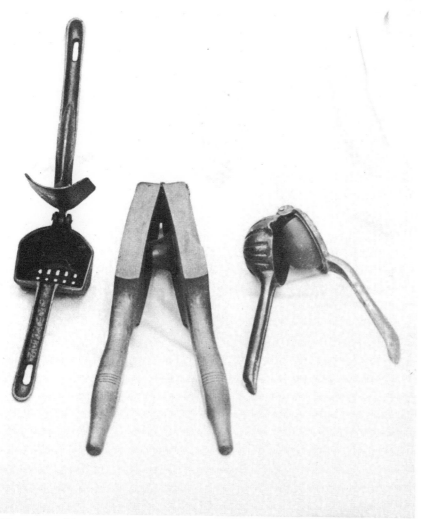

Three types of lemon squeezers

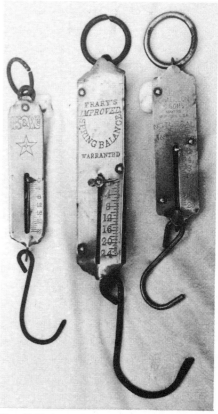

Small kitchen scales with brass fronts

Baskets also played an important role in the kitchen, as they were used to gather eggs, vegetables and other foodstuffs. The old "egg basket," the gizzard or buttocks-shaped basket, was used again to take the eggs and other farm commodities to the general store, where they could be sold or "traded" for necessities—or maybe for a luxury, such as a piece of pattern glass the housewife coveted but couldn't afford. A basket, usually quite large and covered, was used to take food to socials at a neighbor's house or at the church.

Eventually, some ingenious person invented, made, and distributed an individual egg tester or candler. There was quite a problem in those days with egg spoilage, and it was an even greater problem for the housewife who tried to sell a few eggs. She could throw away bad ones she found at home, but selling bad eggs could ruin her reputation.

As important as the mortars and pestles were, the grater was equally essential. First, homemade versions of pierced tin nailed on a wooden board were used to grate corn, then the tinsmith made smaller ones to grate spices like nutmeg. Finally, there were commercially made graters in a variety of styles.

Wooden bowls have been made in all sizes, from tiny to extra large, with the extra large used to mix cornbread and biscuits for harvesting crews. One type of wooden bowl was used more often for working the butter after it was churned. Old-timers still refer to the small, flat examples as "butter bowls" like mother used.

From the earliest days, settlers put a few grains of corn in hot ashes and watched it pop. But manufacturers, ever mindful of the whims of the buying public, devised popcorn poppers. Some were made entirely of tin, while others were made of wire with a tin lid.

Doughnuts could have been and probably were fried in pots of shortening hung on the crane over the fire, but it is known that some were baked, as doughnut irons have been found that closely resemble the waffle irons. There are spaces for three doughnuts to be cooked at one time, and when the dough was put in the irons, the lid was closed, and it was put in the hot coals and ashes.

The Dutch oven, often called a covered spider, was a cooking utensil that made biscuit baking on the coals an easy chore. Some of the spiders had long legs; in fact, most of the early cooking utensils had the long legs that allowed more coals to be piled under the pan.

There are hundreds of other antiques and collectibles associated with cooking in the kitchen. They range from the stoneware crocks and jugs to the later ice tongs. Most of them can still be used in the kitchen, at least in decorative ways. Some of the stoneware is attractive alone, while smaller pieces are attractive when used as containers for dried flowers, a bouquet of fresh flowers, or to hold old tools, such as wooden spoons and rolling pins.

The multi-drawered spice cabinets, both homemade and factory made, are desirable today. The round tin spice boxes are beginning to be collected. After the icebox became a familiar part of the kitchen, ice was delivered by an ice man who used both an ice pick and ice tongs. The picks with advertising are collectible,

The early handmade wooden pitchers have found little use in our modern kitchens except as decorative antiques or containers for dried arrangements. It is surprising how the twentieth-century commercially made tin cooking utensils are showing up in antiques shops and shows. Many of them were given away by manufacturers as a bonus or premium for buying a specific product. One dealer has devised a method of repairing or re-tinning, probably using methods used by the early tinsmiths. It is also a good idea to rub a little cooking oil on old tinware to retard the rusting process. Some collectors with an artistic bend are buying the later tinware and adding beautiful floral or old-time scenic designs.

Tin egg tester

Miniature splint gizzard or buttocks-shaped basket

Gizzard or buttocks-shaped basket, called an egg basket

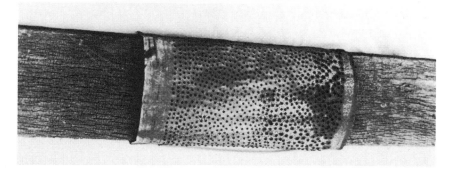

Large early handmade grater

Large splint basket used for harvesting and taking food to socials

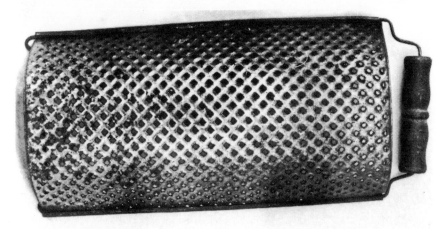

Large, late grater

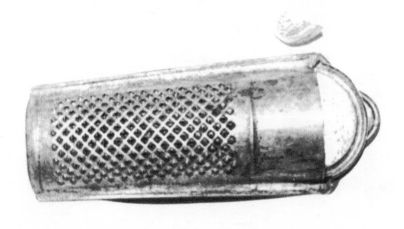

Nutmeg grater

Tin nutmeg grater

Table model grater

Assortment of wooden bowls, dough tray, sifter, and niddy noddy

Wire popcorn popper

Small eight-drawer spice box

Late tin popcorn popper

Doughnut irons

Corn and gourds work well in old dough trays

Dough tray with vegetables and gourds

Dough tray with apples and pomegranate

Wooden buckets, gourd dippers, and bowls and pitchers, used with water kept in the house

Old wooden pitcher with dried arrangement

Although there is a trend by the groups who are going back to live off the land to use the old tools exactly as they were used originally, there are some pieces that defy use today. One is the old wire toaster. In 1910, a toaster was introduced that could toast four slices of bread at one time. It was designed to be used over a flame on the stove. The problem was that the bread had to be turned by hand.

Sausage mills, both the old homemade and the later factorymade examples, can be used on occasion. Other tools falling into that seldom-used category are the noodle cutter, egg separator, and the cherry seeder or pitter.

At one time, cherry pitters or seeders could be found in practically every antiques shop or show one entered. They varied in style from the type that fastened on the table to the table-top model. A decade or so ago someone began making replicas, which ruined the market for collectors.

All the old handmade wooden items are highly sought after. These include the salt boxes, both the wall hanging type and the ones that sat on the table. Iron, copper, and granite ware teakettles are sought after, as are the coffeepots in the same materials. Covered milk pails and cans—especially the granite ware examples—are also collectible, as are the lunch buckets.

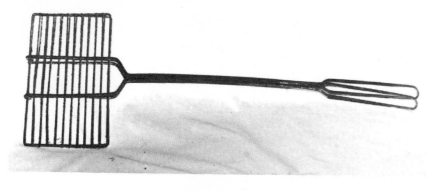

Long-handled wire toaster for use in fireplace

Toaster for use over open flame, circa 1910

Tabletop cherry seeder, a type that has been reproduced

Hanging wooden salt box with missing lid

Cherry seeder that fastened on table

Granite ware milk cans in three sizes

Granite ware over iron Dutch oven

Tin lunch bucket with granite ware top

Teapot made of wood, copper, and brass

Fancy granite ware coffeepot with pewter top

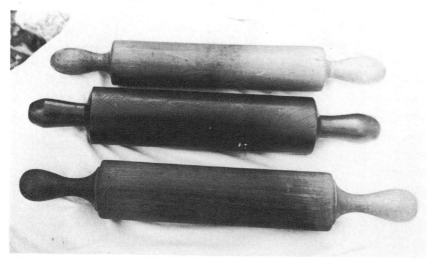

Old wooden rolling pins

Plain granite ware coffeepot

Small hollow wooden rolling pin

Handmade wooden spoons

Wooden spoons displayed in stoneware crock by modern knife holder

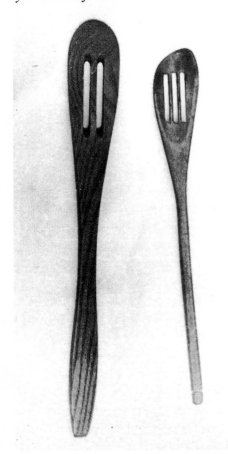

Slotted wooden spoons or stirrers

Assortment of late wooden spoons

The copper ham boiler was popular in Virginia, where settlers were said to have originated a way to perfectly cure pork hams. These hams might be baked, but more often they were boiled in the large copper boilers, then served cold. Later these boilers would be used to boil dirty clothes in areas where it was more feasible to wash a few garments at a time rather than do a big wash outside in freezing weather.

As we have said before, those early settlers didn't waste a thing. For instance, they utilized everything on the hog. The hams were cured, bacon was made from the sides, and the rest was used to make sausages, hogshead cheese, and lard. Even the cooked skins were saved to make "cracklin' bread." To remove all the lard and leave the skins crisp, the settlers made a lard squeezer, with two pieces of wood hinged together on one end and handles shaped on the other. The cooked skins were squeezed between the two boards. Crackling bread is made like cornbread, but with the addition of cracklings.

Another late bloomer in the field of kitchen items was the pie cooler or carrier. It was a wire rack that would hold a half dozen cooling pies in tin or granite ware pie plates. If necessary, it could be carried to socials or church meetings so the pies would not be mashed.

No household chore was as important as preparing meals. In the beginning, settlers lived frugally and the meals weren't anything to brag about. But as time passed, young women were often judged by their culinary skills. For that reason, girls learned "kitchen chores" first and, as with other chores, they were given toy tools and utensils so they could follow along as Mother prepared the meals.

Often the father would whittle a wooden spoon or rolling pin for the girls while he was making one for the mother. Generally, though, the toy kitchen pieces were bought for prices ranging from a few cents to as much as one dollar for the fancy toy woodburning cookstove. There were pewter and tin tea sets to show the girls how to set the table and how to serve the meals. There were also small iron teakettles, coffeepots, the so-called iron bean pots, and short- and long-handled skillets or spiders in several sizes. Toy coffee grinders and eggbeaters were also made, along with a complete set of toy "kitchen cooking utensils," in granite ware.

Copper boiler, favored for cooking Virginia cured hams

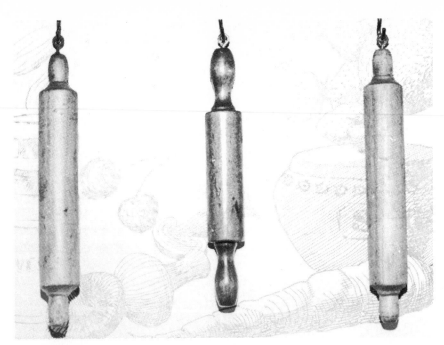

Toy rolling pins

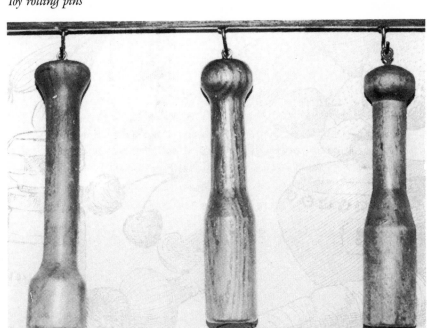

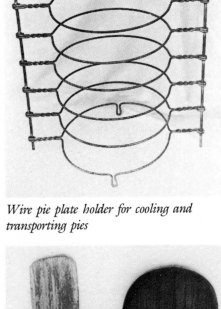

Wire pie plate holder for cooling and transporting pies

Toy stuffers or mashers

Stirrers used in making lard

Handmade lard squeezer or press for making cracklings

Miniature iron Dutch oven

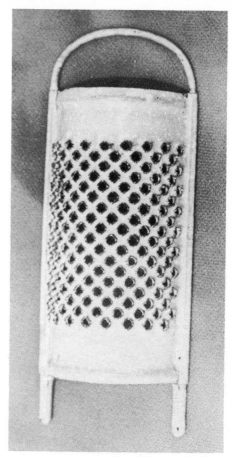

Toy-size granite ware grater

Circa 1910 sausage mill

Miniature china teapot, all that remains of the original tea set

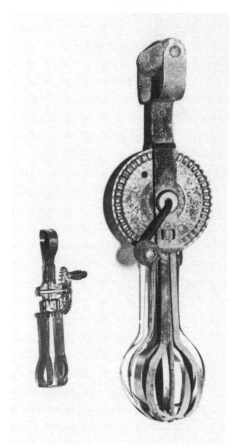

Regular eggbeater with toy size for children

Miniature iron skillets used on toy stoves

Set of miniature granite ware cooking utensils

Toy bean pots, used to teach girls to cook

Toy stove with toy granite ware utensils

Miniature Haviland tureen

Nursery rhyme mugs were a kitchen favorite

Old Staffordshire teapot

Mugs, especially the Mr. Pickwick series, found a place in the kitchen

Early Wedgwood platter

Alphabet plates, used to teach children to read

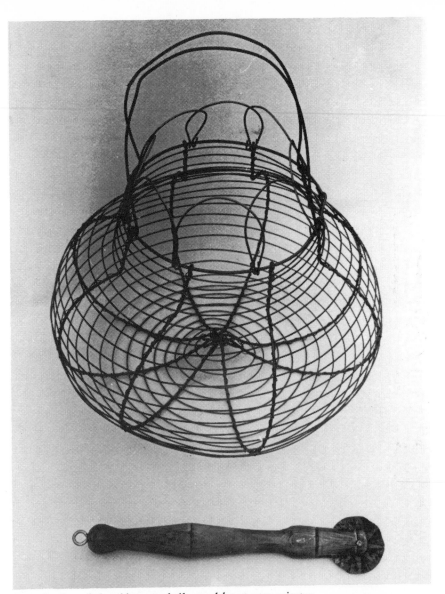

Two late wooden forks

Reproduction of the old potato boiler and late pastry crimper

Late factory-made tinware being sold in antiques shows

Wooden knife box

Early flint glass sugar dish, circa 1850

Later cut-glass coffeepots were filled in the kitchen and taken to the dining room or parlor

Late potato slicer

One-of-a-kind handmade dough or biscuit roller

Bread knife to be used with the board

Wooden bread board for slicing bread

Three tea strainers. One on right is circa 1910 German strainer

Early tin food warmer

Large stoneware crocks, used to make pickles and store butter

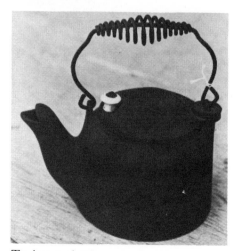

Toy iron teakettle

Old grater decorated for Christmas

Georgia apple cider mill

5

Brew on Thursday

Not only did our ancestors eat heartily, they drank the same way. They were advised not to drink the water in the New World, and apparently they took this advice to heart. Immediately, they began searching for a substitute. They found it in apple cider, a beverage that became so widely used it could have become the first national beverage.

As soon as the settlers figured out which materials would make strong drink, they concocted it. They made metheglin from the locust beans, peachy using peaches, perry made from pears, and various other light beverages from persimmons, elderberries, juniper berries, pumpkins, hickory nuts, sassafras bark, and even walnut tree chips. Later they would make corn and rye whiskey and rum.

The rum, probably the strongest of all the beverages, not only supported the slave trade, but had roots in America, where it was made, and in Africa, where the slaves were sold or traded for shiploads of molasses to be used to make more rum. Most of the old records indicated that rum was made in New England, where there was no demand for slaves. But the rum they made was used to buy some of the slaves that came into the southern plantations.

Few women were involved in the making of hard liquors, but they must have been responsible for keeping enough apple cider for the family. This chore probably would have required a day a week if they were making enough for a large family. They also had to try to preserve enough apples to last from one harvest to the next—enough to prepare the many apple dishes they used, as well as having apples for cider during the year.

Without corn and apples, it is doubtful that the early settlers would have survived. In fact, in looking back over the few dishes they prepared during those early years, it seems they were all made either of corn or apples. They had brought apple seeds with them, as they were aware of the nutrition in apples. Those early apple dishes included puff apple pies and mess apple pies (the difference between the two is unknown), apple tarts, apple slump, apple mose (probably mousse), apple crowdy, apple pan dowdy, and the ever-popular applesauce and apple butter. If the housewife had sufficient cider for the following week, she might want to spend Thursday making applesauce or apple butter, or simply putting apples in storage for future use.

In the 1800s, the best way to preserve apples through the winter was to "Take hard, sound apples; wipe them dry, pack them in tight barrels, putting a layer of bran to each apple so as not to let them touch each other, and they will keep till June." Settlers also suggested keeping the barrels in a cool place, "enveloped in a linen cloth to prevent the apples from freezing."

Apple trees not only furnished food and drink for the pioneers, they also provided wood for various items, including special stirrers. It was said that applesauce and apple butter tasted better when stirred with an apple wood stirrer.

The so-called bedpost dolls, crudely carved wooden dolls made by the early settlers, often were made of apple wood. Apple dolls, those wizened dried-apple-headed dolls, were also made from the fruit. Several types of baskets were closely associated with the harvest and storage of apples. They are referred to as apple baskets.

Small handmade barrel ideal for keeping apples in the kitchen

Short-handled apple butter stirrer, probably used for indoor cooking

Iron pot with apple butter stirrers

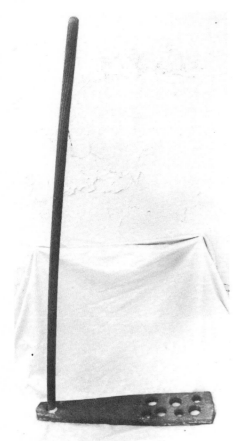

Long-handled stirrer, made for use outside when making apple butter

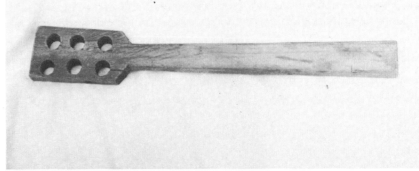

Special stirrer, probably made for applesauce or butter

Apple butter could be made in iron pot or brass kettle. Stirrer and skimmer included

Early on, settlers made cider at home in a cider press and mill. Twenty-five years ago, it was difficult to find a country estate auction that didn't include a cider mill, usually found in the barn. The people continued to use the old mills and presses, although there were commercial cider mills in the more thickly populated areas. The family, usually the men or boys, would deliver their supply of apples to the cider mill, returning later to pick up the cider. It was like the commercial mills that ground the wheat and corn into meal and flour. All were usually powered by water.

When cider was made in quantity like the commercially milled cider, it had to be stored so it would keep. Records on early cider storage are skimpy, but in the mid 1800s it was suggested that the cider be allowed to stand after it came from the cider mill until the pomace settled. It was then put in a "clear vessel" and brought to a boil so the "scum" could be skimmed off carefully. The next step was to put it in "kegs or demijohns," which were then tightly corked or sealed. This method was not only recommended for keeping sweet cider all winter, but it could be kept for several years if it was done correctly. It was brought to the kitchen, one keg at a time, where it could be used as needed.

The apple is responsible for many of the antiques and collectibles found today, including everything from old homemade wooden barrels and kegs to the apple dolls themselves.

Stoneware crocks had many uses, including storing apple butter

Apple cider press

Larger stoneware crocks and a demijohn

Apple cider mill found in mountains

In between those two extremes is a multitude of items, including the old cider mills, presses, apple baskets (both the woven and wire examples), stirrers, brass apple butter kettles, the ever-popular apple peelers that range from the early homemade examples to the later factory-made iron ones, and the stoneware crocks and demijohns used to store the cider. These same demijohns were used later to store and transport the corn whiskey made by the same people who had once drunk only apple cider.

Apples and cider had such a far-reaching effect that some of the pioneers' recipes are still in use today. For instance, in 1865, mulled cider was made by "boiling in a wineglassful and a half of water, a quarter of an ounce of spices (cinnamon, ginger slightly bruised, and clove) with three ounces of fine sugar, until the mixture forms a thick syrup, which must not be allowed to burn— under any circumstances. To avoid this, stir the mixture constantly." As soon as it reached the syrupy consistency, a pint of cider was poured into the syrup and it was stirred gently until it reached the boiling point. It was then served immediately.

Champagne cider was a variation of plain cider. It was made by putting three quarts of spirits (no particular kind was mentioned) and six pounds of honey or sugar into a barrel of good pale cider. It was mixed well and allowed to stand for a fortnight. When a quart of skimmed milk was added, the beverage was ready to be bottled or used.

Wire apple basket, often used in old stores to show off the apples

117

Children might have gathered apples in a vine basket

Homemade apple peeler

Brass apple butter kettle in frame to be used outside

Apple peeler most often found today

Two different types of apple peelers

Thumbprint pattern whiskey tumbler, circa 1860

Tarentum's Virginia whiskey or shot glass, circa 1895

Massachusetts shot glass, part of set that includes rum jug, circa 1895

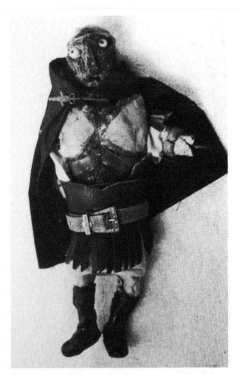

One apple doll emerged as a swashbuckling warrior

Portrait goblet, rarest of the rare goblets, circa 1890

The recipe for spring beer probably shows better than most how the settlers used whatever was available to make whatever they needed or wanted. In the Colonies, where drinking was an art, settlers made spring beer by taking "a small bunch of sweet fern, sarsaparilla, wintergreen, sassafras, prince's pine, cumfrey root, burdock root, nestle root, Solomon's seal, spice bush, and black birch and boiling all or part of them in three or four gallons of water in which two or three ounces of hops and two or three raw potatoes pared and cut in slices had been added." The strength of these was better extracted when boiled in two waters, "for when the liquor is saturated with the hops, it will rather bind up the roots than extract their juices." The roots were boiled for five or six hours, then the liquor was strained. The last step was adding a quart of molasses to each three gallons of beer. It was said that half a loaf of brown bread could be added to the beer to make it rich. If the liquor was too thick, cold water was added to dilute it. When it was lukewarm, a pint of fresh, lively yeast was added. It was then placed in a "temperate situation," and covered, but not so tightly as to retard fermentation. After fermentation it was either bottled or kept in a tight keg.

When the brewing, storing, or apple butter and sauce making was completed, the mother often saved out some choice apples to use for apple dolls. They really weren't complicated to make, but the quality and beauty of the finished product depended to a great extent on the mother's talents and skill as well as the available materials for dressing the dolls.

More talent was necessary in dressing the doll than in the actual making, as the apple was going to dry in its own peculiar way regardless of a woman's skills. She could improve it with practice, as this would teach her the best ways to cut the features. Clothes make the man, it has been said, and it was never more true than in the case of an apple doll. With imagination and ingenuity the mother could create a princess, a warrior, or a little old gray-haired lady. Since apples were plentiful and free for the taking, the mother might prepare a dozen or more at the same time—more if she had lots of daughters.

To make the apple dolls, the largest apples were selected and peeled, then a dowel made from a short limb was inserted into the center of the apple. This limb or dowel would later become the framework for the doll's body. Deep holes were cut in the apple to form the eyes, and the nose and mouth were blocked in. As the apple began to dry and shrink, two glass beads were implanted for eyes. The beads could be placed with the solid side showing, in which case a dot of black could be added for the pupil. Or the hole in the bead could be in front. The hole would be filled with stove black to achieve the same results.

After the child had selected the head she liked best, a wax or stocking body was attached to the dowel, and the doll dressed in whatever style of clothing was available. The finishing touches included a touch of color on the cheeks and lips and a wig made of yarn. The color of the yarn wig was chosen to fit the face—gray for the older dolls and black for the younger looking ones.

Apple dolls are still being made today, simply by following the same steps as those used by the pioneer mother. An additional step has been added lately. Since the apples continue to shrink for a long time, makers now brush the head with clear varnish after the drying is well advanced to help slow the process.

Apple dolls weren't the only apple-related item for the children. They might also have miniature wine sets or toy size decanters and wine glasses. In fact, drinking of all kinds from the cider through the hard liquors to the later lemonade created the need for all types of drinking glasses. The glass companies were delighted to oblige, and they made goblets, cordials, champagnes (both the stemmed and the flat-bottomed, or champagne tumbler), wines or wine glasses, and whiskey tumblers or shot glasses, as well as decanters and rum jugs.

Miniature Fickle Block pattern decanter and wines, circa 1895

Imitation cut glass decanter in pressed glass, circa 1900

Lincoln Drape flint glass wine, circa 1860

121

Wooden churn with hickory bands

6
Churn on Friday

If corn kept the Pilgrims alive during those first few difficult years, the cow should be credited with furnishing them with other necessities well into the 1800s.

Oxen provided the manpower to clear the fields and then pulled the logs cleared from those fields to the cabin site to build a home. Hitched to a plow rather than a log, they plowed the fields so the pioneers could plant and cultivate the foods necessary to keep them alive. They also pulled the wagon or cart to move the family from one area to another, and they pulled the wagon that took settlers to church on Sunday.

The female cows gave milk used for drinking and making butter and cheese. Later, settlers would learn how to use the milk to make ice cream that could be molded in pewter molds. Young male calves and older cows that were past the calf and milk producing stage were slaughtered to furnish beef and veal for the family. Beef and veal began to replace venison as the staple meat product.

Hides were saved and cured to make shoes or chair seats, while the horns were made into drinking cups or powder horns to hold the black powder needed for the muzzleloaders.

The need for oxen decreased as houses were made of sawed lumber or clapboard and horses and mules replaced them in the fields. Drinking glasses and cups began to be made of pewter, and settlers learned how to bottom chairs with oak splints. The new guns used bullets, so the need for powder horns decreased. But the market for beef and veal continued, while the demand for milk, butter, cheese, and ice cream increased.

With modern machinery it is a short process from udder to butter. But in the days of churning it could take several days. The milk had to be strained and put in the churn, where it was allowed to sour. A day or two later, it was beaten or churned for an hour or so, until the butter rose to the top. Then the butter was "taken up" and put into a wooden bowl where the milk was "worked" out of it. Only after it was allowed to cool sufficiently could it be molded in the old wooden butter molds. Later there would be glass and metal butter molds and butter prints, but early on, they were all made of wood, with some of the most desirable ones hand carved. The first known patent for a butter mold was issued April 17, 1866.

Today molds with a design of a cow, hearts, eagle, thistle, swan, or pineapple are the most sought after, while those with a lathe-turned wheat or floral design are not as desirable. In the early days, butter molds were a work of art. Some of the old ones identified the farm where the butter was made. A swan design might signify a farm by a river, while a cow might indicate a small dairy. Some of the handmade ones will be found with the initials of the maker and the date, but these are rare.

It is doubtful that any of the butter that sold for three pence, or about three pennies a pound, back in 1740 was molded, but it was described as sweet and good tasting. Cheese was described as "neither cheap nor good," but as any cheese aficionado knows, cheese making has to be worked out with the climate and temperature.

Milk had been an important part of the diets in the Old Country, so it was only natural it would continue in popularity as soon as cows arrived in the Colonies. In 1725, articles in the Boston newspaper listed bread and milk as the foods most often eaten at breakfast and supper.

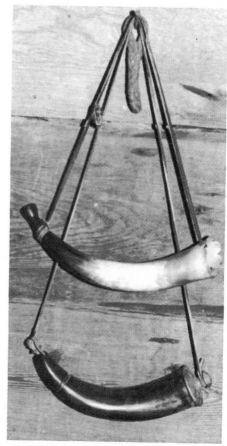

Powder horn and hunting horn used to call the dogs

Nearly a century earlier, a minister had written that ministers and milk were the only cheap things in New England. At that time, milk sold for about a penny a quart. Apparently things hadn't changed much by 1735, when another minister was asked about the menu of his family. For breakfast and supper, he said, they only had milk and bread, but for lunch they might have hasty pudding and milk, stewed pumpkin and milk, baked apples and milk, or berries with milk.

Milk and butter, whether from a domestic cow, a goat, or a water buffalo, is known and used throughout the world. It was said that even though the women in Egypt were not allowed to go outside the house a century or so ago, they still had cows that slept in the huts with them. They also had a different method of churning. They fashioned a goatskin and filled it half full of milk, hung it on a peg, and jerked it back and forth until the butter appeared. They then drained it, but didn't wash or salt it before using it to cook rice with butter.

Milk was avoided in the mourning customs of at least one country. As late as 1880, Arabian women stained their hands and feet with indigo and allowed it to remain for eight days. During that time they refused to use milk in any way, on the grounds that its white color "does not accord with the gloom of our minds."

Unusual homemade churn dasher

Round crank-type churn

Wooden churn with brass bands

Crank-type churn

Paddles from crank churn

Later brass churn

125

Large crank-type churn

Swinging churn

Churning was done by pulling handle back and forth

Large molds, often called printers

Commercial size butter mold used by early
small dairies

Three sizes of wooden butter bowls

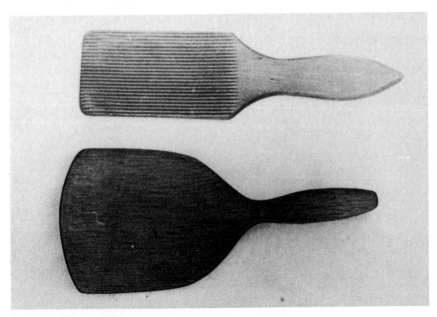

Butter paddles or ladles

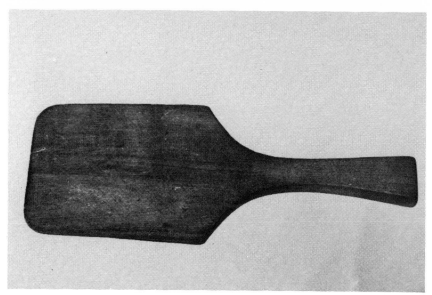

Butter spades

Homemade and machine-made butter ladles

Part of old butter mold

Early butter mold

129

Sought-after molds and prints with swan, eagle, and shield

Pineapple-design butter mold

Hotel butter mold

Late butter mold

Late daisy design

Three late, plain butter molds

Granite ware butter dish

Glass butter dish with reclining cow on top

Back in the Colonies, women were experimenting with ways to preserve excess milk and butter. Without an icehouse, about the only way to save milk was to let it sour and make butter and buttermilk. A favorite way of keeping the milk cool for serving at mealtime was to put it in a milk pail and lower it into the water in the well. It was taken out at mealtime or when fresh milk was needed for cooking. The housewife was always careful to rotate it, as it could sour in the well.

To preserve butter or to keep it during the winter or when the cow was dry, the housewife began saving extra butter every time she churned. There were a couple of ways she could save it, but she needed at least six pounds each time she began to "pot" it. Into this freshly churned butter she would add one spoonful each of sugar, salt, and saltpeter. After this was well mixed, she would put it in a stoneware crock, alternating layers of butter and salt, but it was never covered so tightly as to exclude the air.

Some preferred to put the butter in a brine solution made of salt, plus a spoonful of saltpeter to each two gallons of water. Another method was to salt the butter lightly using a half ounce of salt to each pound of butter, and let it remain out for a day or two. Then a mixture of four ounces of salt, two ounces of loaf sugar, and a quarter of an ounce of saltpeter was mixed together, then mixed in the butter. Using this method, the butter was packed in muslin and then in crocks or tubs.

Unless the family was able to save their extra butter, they could face a three-month period of no butter. Often they had neighbors with whom they could swap butter, but most preferred not to take that chance. Instead, they tried to pot their butter and save it, but sometimes the butter became old or "tainted" despite all their efforts. Not being a wasteful people, they had ways to "restore the sweetness." One method was to cut the butter into small pieces and put it in a churn with enough new milk to churn it again. After sufficient churning, it was difficult to tell the old from the new, they said.

Several factors are important in making cheese, according to the old-timers. One is the temperature of the milk when it is first warmed in the tub. It should never be hotter than when it first comes from the cow's udder, otherwise it will be tough. Two ways of breaking curds have a great bearing on the taste. The first, and the one that is supposed to make the best tasting cheese, is to gather the curds gently in your hand, then press them gently against the sides of the tub, allowing the whey to pass through the fingers until it becomes clear. It then is ladled off. The other method is to break the curds and gather the whey. These may seem insignificant, but old cheesemakers swear that the gentle touch made the best cheese.

They also had different ways of salting the cheese. Some vowed that one was better than the other, but like modern recipes, it all probably depended on the taste of the individual.

The consensus of opinion gathered from old records is that the majority of cheeses made in the New World were excellent. Of course, there is always the possibility that the settlers were hungry enough that anything would have tasted good. But it stands to reason that if they came from cheesemaking countries, they would soon have adjusted their recipes and methods to those of the northern colonies.

Cheesemaking, like churning, was a time-consuming chore, beginning with the housewife putting the milk near the fire to curdle, breaking the curds, and separating them from the whey. The next step was to tie the curds into a cheesecloth and put it in a cheese basket, a hexagon woven basket, that rested on a cheese ladder over a tub. The cheese was then put in a cheese press, which was a large wooden contraption. After pressing, it was put back on the cheese ladder, where it was rubbed, turned, and allowed to age.

The use of milk didn't stop there. It was used in candymaking, especially in the chocolates that were molded in both pewter and tin molds.

Cheese press

Cheese tester

Homemade cheese basket

Ice cream is believed to have been made first on a limited basis in the eighteenth century. The sweetened milk was put into pewter or copper molds, then frozen in the icehouses that were part of the large northern farms.

By the nineteenth century, the popularity of ice cream was growing. Like most things in the New World, it was never finished. People continued to experiment in hopes of finding a better taste or a better method. This applied to ice cream as well, and in 1864, Nancy Johnson invented the first ice cream freezer. Little is known about this first freezer, but chances are it was fashioned after the old butter churn. Women had found that if they beat or churned the ice cream mixture before freezing it, it was much smoother. The first freezer, then, probably had an inside container to hold the ice cream mixture while an outside container held the ice that had been cut from the pond and stored in the icehouse.

It is not unusual today to see the old wooden bucket ice cream freezers in antiques shows and shops, as they are fast becoming qualified antiques. By 1904 there was an abundance of ice cream freezers being offered by numerous companies. That year, McIntosh Hardware Corporation, Cleveland, Ohio, offered eight types of freezers made by four different companies: White Mountain, Peerless Iceland, Freezo, and Artic. A large model "with fly wheel for hotel and confectioners' use" could be bought in sizes that were measured by quarts. The fifteen-quart size sold for $21, the twenty-quart size for $28, and the twenty-five-quart size listed for $35.

"A triple motion, Samson power freezer with tight and loose pulley" that would make forty quarts at a time sold for $150. The family size freezers ranged from the two-quart size selling for $3 to $4 each to the eight-quart size priced at $7 to $9 each. They were described as heavily tinned, especially on "the part that comes in contact with the cream," while the outside was galvanized.

Ice cream freezer shown in 1904 catalogue

Candy and ice cream molds in a variety of designs

Late candy molds

Pewter molds for candy and ice cream

In the same catalogue, there was an ice cream "disher" or scoop that was apparently made to be used exclusively in confectioners' shops. Made in five different sizes, they measured so many dips per quart. The largest, or the five-dips-to-a-quart size, sold for $3.50 a dozen, while the smaller twelve-dips-to-a-quart sold for $2.40 a dozen. Even the dishers or scoops were geared to the quart. There is no explanation for the prices unless so much less material was used to make the smaller size.

The origin of the ice cream cone is attributed to an Italian immigrant named Italo Marchiony, who reportedly began making and selling cones as early as 1856, but did not obtain a patent until 1903. The popularity of the ice cream cone began in earnest with the 1904 World's Fair in St. Louis, where a vendor named Ernest Hamwi was selling waffles next to a man selling ice cream. The ice cream man ran out of dishes, so the waffle maker began rolling thin waffles and shaping them into cornucopias or cones. As they cooled, they hardened to a delicious crispness. The ice cream man began selling his cream in the waffle cones, and a new industry was born. A Portland, Oregon, man named Fred Bruckman obtained a patent in 1910 for what is believed to be the first ice cream cone-making machine.

Milk was also the inspiration for many china and glass antiques, such as cheese dishes and creamers or cream pitchers. The cheese needed protection from flying insects, and what better way than to keep it in a beautiful cheese dish, often shaped like a wedge of cheese. It was great for serving as well as storing.

It became fashionable to serve milk or cream for coffee or fruit in attractive cream pitchers. More often than not they came in sets of a creamer and matching sugar dish. People could buy whatever they wanted, but the most desirable sets were those available around the turn of the present century. They consisted of a creamer, sugar, spooner, and butter dish.

Along with the miniature butter molds that were used to make individual servings of butter for large dinner parties, most of the miniatures in the milk department were toy size table sets consisting of a creamer, sugar, spooner, and butter dish; and the water sets, including a pitcher and a six tumblers or goblets.

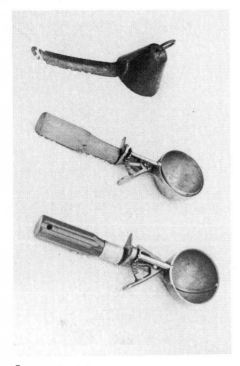

Ice cream scoops

Wedgwood cheese dish

Cream pitcher with applied leaves and berries

Wedge-shaped cheese dish

Creamer that was also a measure, circa 1890, with Scroll and Daisy pattern

Milk glass creamers in Grape and Cherry pattern, circa 1890

Rare creamer in Bullet-Emblem pattern, circa 1898

137

Toy Pattee Cross pitcher and two tumblers, circa 1910

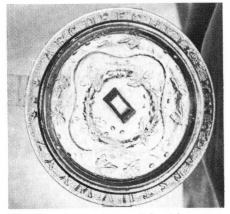

Wee Branches toy butter dish with alphabet around edge, circa 1900

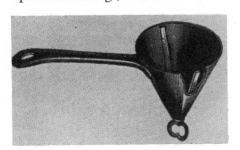

Tinned ice cream disher from 1904 catalogue

Miniature creamer and sugar in Grape with Ovals pattern, circa 1895

138

7
Mend on Saturday

It was probably apropos in the early days to set aside one day for mending, as clothing was scarce and materials to weave new ones even scarcer. But by 1644, there were an estimated three thousand sheep in the colony of Massachusetts alone, and the number was growing fast.

The settlers had found flax growing when they arrived, but they lacked the necessary tools to make it into fabric. This was remedied in time. Since most settlers were from England, they naturally preferred the wools they were accustomed to. Sheep were allowed to graze on the commons, and if a dog killed a sheep, the owner had to hang his dog and pay the owner of the sheep twice the cost of the animal. Eating lamb and mutton was not allowed.

Other colonies also worked hard to increase their sheep population. Virginians offered six pounds of their treasured tobacco for any yard of homespun woolen fabric made by a person living in the area. A pound of tobacco was offered for a pair of woolen socks made at home.

Linen was made from flax, which was easy to grow, but required long hours of hard work to prepare it for the loom. Flax seed as sown in May, and by July the plants were grown, ready to be pulled up by the roots and laid out to dry. Once the flax was dry, it was "rippled," as a coarse wooden comblike tool with heavy iron teeth was worked back and forth through the tops to loosen and remove the seeds for next year's planting. This work was usually done by the men and boys.

Once the seeds were out, the flax plants were tied into bundles to dry even more. A few weeks to a month later, they were considered dry enough. Then the stalks or bundles were watered so the leaves would rot away and the fiber inside the stalks would soften. The settlers usually put the stalks in a stream or pond for four or five days. This posed a problem in the ponds, as the rotting flax would poison the fish. In a running stream, however, the fish survived. Many early settlers built their homes near a spring or stream to eliminate carrying water for long distances.

In about a week, the flax was ready to be taken out of the water and dried. The next step was to put the flax on the flax-brake so the fibers inside could be removed.

Even after this hard, time-consuming work, the flax was not yet ready for spinning, as it had to be "swingled," or run through a swingling block and knife to remove all the remaining particles of bark. Sometimes it was swingled twice to improve the fibers, even though refuse from the swingling was not discarded. It was saved to make coarse thread for weaving bags or work clothes.

Now it was time to "beetle" the flax, or put it in a contraption resembling a mortar and beating it with a pestle. The next step was hackling or hatcheling, where the flax was "combed" into long threads while the short fibers were combed out. To make fine linen fabric, the flax might be hackled as many as a half dozen more times before it was ready for the spinning wheel.

As early as the ninth century, spinning was an honorable occupation for women. Spinsters or spinners worked regularly going from one home to another, wherever they were needed and would be paid. Spinster thus became the name used for unmarried women.

Flax wheel with quilt in background

Although the flax might now be spun into thread, the long chore of preparing it for the loom was not yet completed. The thread would be wound into skeins on a yarn winder, also called a clock reel. When it was removed, it was ready to be bleached.

The bleaching process began by putting the skeins in water that was changed regularly for four or five days. Each time the water was changed, the skeins were squeezed as nearly dry as possible. At the end of this time, they were taken back to the stream of running water, where they were washed repeatedly "until the water ran clean." Then it was time for them to be "bucked." For this chore, the skeins of thread were put in a bucking tub and bleached with ashes and hot water. Sometimes the spinner might use slaked lime and buttermilk; one method might work better for one while another worked better for someone else. During the years, each person worked out the method that produced the finest, whitest linen thread.

Once the bleaching process was out of the way, the thread was again put in clear water for about a week. When the week was over, it was time to wash, rinse, and dye the thread. Softer colors were used for the linen than for wool. Whether it was flax, wool, or cotton, the thread or yarn was usually dyed with roots, bark, or berries indigenous to the area.

Like the spinning and weaving of the wool, the flax also created jobs for many people. There were few jobs for young ladies in those early days except as maids, but they could go from one home to another to help the housewife spin thread for her loom. It was said that at least a half dozen or more spinsters or spinners were required to keep enough thread for one weaver. In the 1700s, the average pay for a spinner was eight cents a day, provided she could spin as much as two skeins of thread a day. She was also given free room and board while in the home.

Not only was there work for the young ladies in spinning and weaving, there was work for the men as well. Many men would take their looms and go from house to house weaving, much as the girls had done with their spinning. And in those early days in New England, men made spinning wheels. They were called wheelwrights just like the later wagon wheel makers. In both cases, they had to be skilled enough to make a perfect wheel. The early wheelwrights had to make wheels for the spinning wheel that would run absolutely true so the thread would be even and strong.

By the 1800s, many men were building spinning wheels and yarn winders for their families. Some of the more skilled even made some for the neighbors. In the mountain areas, a skilled craftsman often sold spinning wheels and wool yarn winders for a dollar each, but in New England the wheelwrights are reported to have sold their flax wheels for a dollar, while their clock-reel or winder and wool wheels sold for two dollars each.

Flax hatchel

Different type of flax wheel

Thus, it is understandable why there is such a wide choice of spinning wheels and yarn winders available today. Some of the winders are actually quite crude, but this gives them "character."

Two of the old sayings that originated with the wool industry are still in use. "It's all wool and a yard wide" probably originated with the early fabrics to denote that it was made entirely of wool, not a mixture of wool and flax, and that it was a yard wide. Now it indicates that the product, not necessarily of wool, is excellent quality and is what it is represented to be. "Dyed in the wool" used to refer to a dye process that required much skill and was a better process than that used to dye the thread. Now it is used to describe people who are "set in their ways."

The wool industry gave the early settlers much more than old sayings. It gave them jobs, and it furnished warm clothing for the hard New England winters. Preparing the wool was easier and not nearly as time consuming as preparing the flax, but it did require work and a certain amount of skill.

Generally the men sheared the sheep, but on occasion the women were known to take over the job. Once the wool was cut or sheared, the ladies had to go through it with deft fingers, sorting out the tarred or branded wool. The pure white wool was put in bags to be dyed, but the damaged wool was not discarded. It was saved to be spun and woven into the coarser fabrics.

Another style of flax wheel

Much more wool than flax was dyed. Blue was the favorite color and was used in varying shades from a dark navy blue to a pale sky blue. All the blue shades were obtained from indigo.

Madder, cochineal, and logwood made the various reds. Madder made a durable, but not brilliant, red. The bark of the oak and hickory made browns, and yellow came from the bark of the sassafras. With the right combination, an orange dye could be made from the sassafras.

The early settlers preferred black, brown, or gray. To make a slate color, they used tea leaves set with copperas, or sugar loaf paper with vinegar and set with alum. For a light gray, probably for summer wear, they used the bark of white maple with alum.

The dying of the wool was a bit complicated, but nothing to compare with preparing flax. The wool was dyed, dried, and maybe dyed again, and it was always rinsed thoroughly. When the correct color was attained, the wool was ready for carding. Apparently the dyeing and all the washing and rinsing took some of the natural oils out of the wool, because old-timers say it had to be greased again with about three pounds of grease to each ten pounds of wool before it was carded.

Wool cards, like cotton cards, resemble paddles with handles. The wool cards had coarse wires, while the cotton cards had finer wires. Until around 1650, wool cards were entirely handmade in the home.

Wool cards

Cotton cards

Homemade yarn winder or clock reel

Generally the work was done by the man, but could be done by the women. First, the leather back of the card had to be pierced with an awl so the wire teeth could be inserted. They were then cut off, bent slightly, and fastened into place. In 1667, a Massachusetts company began selling wire made especially for wool cards, and by 1784 a machine had been invented that could cut and bend 36,000 wires per hour. Another machine was invented to pierce the holes in the leather backs. The biggest chore was inserting and fastening the wire in the leather. The women took it over as their own, as it allowed them to work at home and make a little extra money.

In 1880, a man named Amos Whittemore invented a machine that would make a wool card in one operation. This, of course, hurt the part-time workers, who were still making a few wool cards at home.

Actually Whittemore's machine was needed at the time, as spinning and weaving machines were being built, and there just weren't enough handmade cards to keep thread for the mills. In a few years they, too, became obsolete after a carding machine was invented in England. It soon found its way into the mills in America.

After the wool was carded into fleecy rolls ready for spinning, it could either be spun as soft yarn or combed with the wool comb, if hand-twisted yarn was needed. Most wool combs were approximately 12″ long and had about thirty wire teeth. Balls of fleecy wool were drawn through the teeth. Like working the flax, this eliminated everything but the finest wool, but the wool that was combed out was used to make a coarse thread for weaving less desirable fabrics. The combed wool was used for making the finest garments, and in diaries, Colonists mentioned the fine quality of wool being made—fine enough to equal that made in England.

To spin flax, the spinster could sit or stand, but to spin wool she had to stand. Not only did she stand, but she took three steps and back in a movement that could only be compared to a dance step. It was said that the spinning wheel hummed its own tune, and the spinsters kept step to it. In the early days, spinsters used a distaff instead of the spinning wheel, but they could spin more thread on the wheel.

Before the advent of the mills, the making of wool fabric in the home furnished the family with all their needs. They were able to make a little extra money by making fabric to be sold. In those early days there were about as many men as women weaving. In winter, the whole family worked on their wool. The father might weave, the mother spin, and the boys and girls carded the wool. The older girls would help with the spinning and wind the yarn on the niddy noddy or yarn winder.

The collector will find a variety of styles to choose from when selecting an old instrument used to wind yarn. They were usually handmade and were made in a variety of styles and materials.

The niddy noddy was described in a little verse the children learned at school, ''Niddy noddy, niddy noddy, two heads and one body.'' That describes the tool rather well, as it had a body or rod with bars set in opposite directions on either end. It has been said that more skill was required to wind the yarn on the niddy noddy than on the yarn winder, because the yarn had to be wound with a waving, somewhat jerky motion so it could be removed easily.

Often a weaver used a swift to fill both the quills for the weft and the spools for the warp. It could be fastened on a table or chair where the yarn could be put on the swift or removed as the swift rapidly rotated. Swifts were like baskets in that they could be made by sailors on long sea voyages. They were made as gifts for the wife or girlfriend back home. Some of the swifts were plain wooden affairs, while others were works of art made of ivory and inlaid with mother of pearl.

At one time, the spinning wheel was taken apart and carried on horse-back to the neighbor's house so the ladies could spin the day together, yet not waste the time with idle chatter. Eventually looms were transported the same way. In fact, there was a time a century or so ago when weavers would stay at a customer's home for weeks, or until they had woven as much fabric as the family needed for the time being. They also made woven coverlets and fabric for household linens, quilts, bedspreads, sheets, or curtains. Weavers were welcomed not only for the work they did but to bring news of other households.

There were large looms, usually built by the man in the family or by the local loom maker from oak or pine. The shuttles were made of boxwood, dogwood, or applewood. These large looms were used for making yard-wide woolens or sections of coverlets. Then there were the many smaller looms, such as the tape-looms, braid looms, garter looms, and gallus looms or frames.

Belts were not as plentiful in those days; in fact, they were notoriously scarce. Men wore galluses or suspenders to hold up their pants.

Cotton, although one of the earliest fabric materials, was one of the last to be used in the Colonies. This probably stems from the fact that cotton was not as well known in Europe as in Egypt or India, where it had been grown and woven into fabric centuries before America was discovered. Exactly when cultivation began is unknown, but mummies have been found wrapped in cotton fabric. Some of the early history of India indicates cotton was being planted and woven there at least eight centuries before the birth of Christ. When the cotton name began to be used is unknown. It is known, however, that Pliny referred to it in some of his writings as a ''shrub which we call 'gossypium' and others 'xylon' from which stuffs are made that we call 'xylina'.''

An early chronicler described cotton as ''plants with real flesh and blood lambs growing upon a short stem flexible enough to allow the lamb to feed upon the surrounding grass.'' Apparently he was unable to believe that a plant could produce anything other than wool—if it was being used to make fabric. Another described cotton as ''a tree bearing seed-pods which bursting when ripe disclose within little lambs with soft fleece which Scythians use for weaving into clothing.''

Spinster stood while working this wheel

Yarn winder

Homemade two-spool yarn winder

Homemade yarn winder

Coverlet

Name of maker, but no date

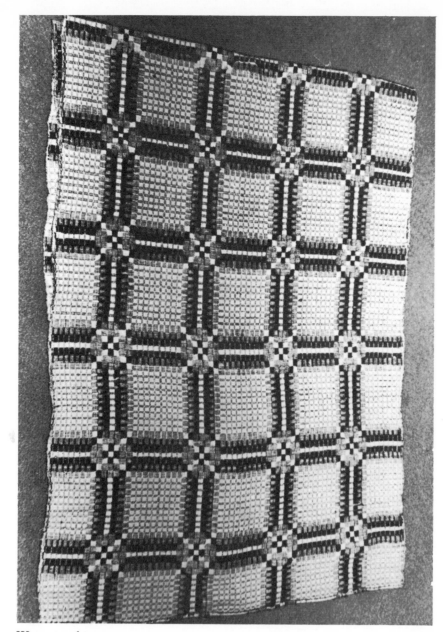

Woven coverlet

Floral design coverlet

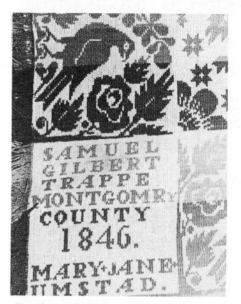

Coverlets with birds or eagles are desirable

*Coverlets with the name of the weaver
and the date are more desirable*

There are several logical reasons why cotton was a late bloomer in the Colonies. The first thing was the fact most of the pioneers settled in the New England area, moving on later to Virginia and into Georgia. A warm, humid climate and sandy land are required to grow cotton. Neither was available in any of the Colonies except south Georgia. Another was the removal of the seed, which was an even more horrendous task than working the flax. The plentiful cotton seeds had to be removed one seed at a time. And once the seeds were out, it was next to impossible to spin thread hard enough to make good fabric. It had to be mixed with linen.

In 1792, Eli Whitney invented the cotton gin, a machine that could separate the seeds from the cotton, and the manufacture of cotton fabric was on its way in the Colonies. In 1767, James Hargreaves invented a spinning jenny that at first would only spin one thread at a time like a spinning wheel, but later it was improved to spin as many as thirty threads at a time into good cotton fabric.

Woman working an early ribbon loom

Small loom

Large loom to make yard widths

Old habits are hard to break, and the settlers continued to spin and weave their own fabrics. One reason was probably the cost. It cost hard cash to buy fabric that had been made by the machines, but it didn't cost anything but time and labor to make fabric at home. As late as the 1950s, women in the mountains were still weaving on the old looms that had been passed down from one generation to the next. At that time, they were weaving mostly rugs, place mats, or towels to be sold in the gift shops in the nearby resort towns.

Early on, they had two choices of floor covering. The first was the stenciled floor cloth, and the other was a rug made out of scraps or worn-out clothing. The habit of making one's own rugs continued long after all types of rugs became available in the marketplace. The women continued to save worn-out clothing to weave their "rag" rugs or to make braided rugs.

The housewife not only made rugs for her floors, but was responsible for making the curtains, bedspreads, coverlets, tablecloths, napkins, and other household linens. The linens went into a girl's dowry chest, along with quilts.

Quilting has been known for thousands of years—not the patchwork-type quilting that became known as an American folk art, but quilted clothing like that worn under suits of armor. The Chinese are believed to have been the first to wear the quilted clothing under their armor, while other countries used the quilted pieces for various purposes, from capes to floor coverings.

148

Pioneers decided not to waste the scraps of fabric left over from making their clothing. They also refrained from throwing away the remaining portions of worn garments. Whatever the reason, they used these tiny scraps to develop the patchwork quilt that is now one of the most popular and expensive of antiques.

Thought to have originated in the early 1700s, quilts went on to become one of the most popular types of needlework. In the early days, the quilt was used as a cover for the bed to provide warmth and as a covering for the windows and doors to stop the flow of cold air through loosely fitted openings.

Some want to believe the quilt was designed so the housewife could have something colorful in her otherwise drab home. The first homes and many of the later ones were extremely dull and drab, as they were built of logs that only turned darker with age. The smoke from the open fireplace added to the dull, dark color. Colorful appointments were practically unknown. So, in an effort to not only utilize scraps of fabric and to add color, they began making patchwork quilts.

Originally women used wool for the batting or padding. It was the only material available and it was used for warmth. Later some women would use a mixture of wool and cotton, and finally cotton seemed to be the favorite. In the mountain areas where there were no gins, the housewife still planted a few rows of cotton in the garden to be used for batting in her quilts. It was difficult to remove the seeds, so some of the ingenious husbands made crude cotton gins out of two wooden rollers with handles. This contraption was fixed on a wooden base. Apparently, no one tried to patent the idea, and each man continued to build the gin as he thought it would work best. Several different examples have been found to confirm this.

The pioneer woman's work was long and time-consuming, limiting her social life. Church on Sunday was about the extent of her social life, except for a quilting bee now and then. A dozen ladies might gather at the home of a neighbor to help "get out" or finish a quilt. During the fall they would go from one house to another, spending the day talking and quilting. It was a welcome break from the regular, monotonous household chores.

During this time, some of the ladies who were artistically inclined began designing quilt patterns. Later they would buy new fabric for some quilts so they could have the same colors throughout. But in the early days, they used whatever they had. As others saw the designs, they began to borrow them and add small changes they thought would make an improvement in the overall design. Slight variations will be noticed in some quilts with the same name.

Perhaps the most beautiful of the old quilts are the so-called crazy quilts, made of scraps of velvet, brocade, or satin. The fabric alone is enough to make them rich looking, but the makers usually went a step further. They did fancy stitchery on and around each piece in the quilt. The majority used a briarstitch, using a heavy thread so it would really stand out. The briarstitch was done around each and every piece in the quilt, as well as around the border. In various pieces there may have been a spidery flower or flowers worked in various colors of the same type thread.

Embroidery developed around the eleventh century in the monasteries and convents in Europe. At first it was so elaborately and intricately done, it was only used in the church. Realizing the beauty of the work, as well as the time required to make it, the monks and nuns decided to train others. They began taking children into the convents to teach them the intricacies of the work. As the children learned and went back out into the world, they taught others, but for several centuries the needlework was used only in the church and worn by nobility. In some countries, there were laws against anyone else wearing it.

Mountain-made cotton gin

Handmade cotton gin

Patchwork quilt, Broken Star pattern

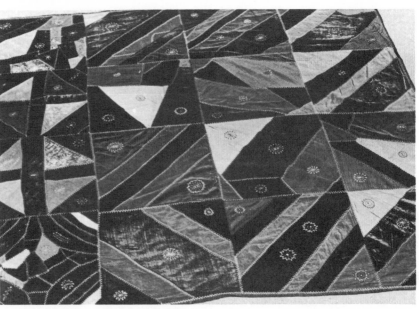

Velvet crazy quilt with fancy stitchery

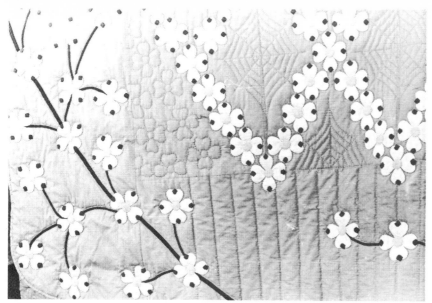

Appliquéd quilt with dogwoods

Fancy quilting is as desirable as the design.

Intricately designed appliqué quilt

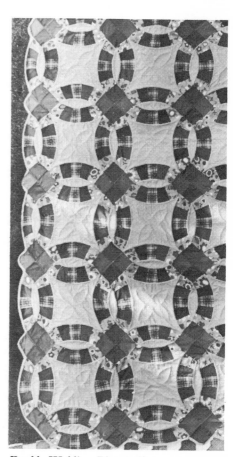

Double Wedding Ring quilt

Naturally, this restriction only made embroidery more desirable. Children continued to be taught to do the various stitches, beginning when they were five and six years old. Loara Standish, daughter of Miles Standish, worked on her sampler while living aboard the *Mayflower,* waiting for the family home to be built in the New World.

In the Colonies, the ladies from the richer European families had more time to work on their fancy stitchery, but the poorer folk had to work whenever they could find the time or the material. Many worked on household linens at night while sitting around the fire. The young girls worked whenever they had a chance, even taking their sewing with them when they went to visit friends. That way they didn't waste any time, as they could sew while they talked. Most of this time they were making household linens for their dower chests.

The old "cubberd cloths" and other linens of the early days would be difficult to find today, but there are plenty of linens, monogrammed towels, antimacassars, centerpieces, tablecloths, napkins, and doilies from the Victorian Era. Interest in old linens and in clothing is increasing—and so are prices.

In the mid-1800s the sewing machine was introduced and the chore of clothing the family became much easier.

Late sampler

Cross-stitched bookmark

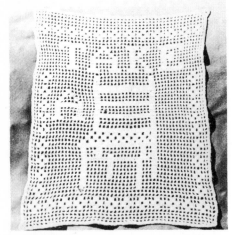

Antimacassar from the Victorian Era

Centerpiece with crocheted lace border

Monogrammed towel with drawn-work border

Dower chest with 1783 date

Eighteenth-century walnut dower chest

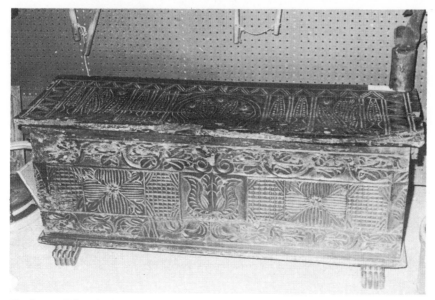

Early English oak chest

Hoop skirt with similar dress for daughter

8

Go to Church on Sunday

The Pilgrims had come to the New World seeking religious freedom, and they weren't about to accept compromises. They began their worship services in the Colonies' first fort.

They were also adamant about leaving some of the old religious customs and names behind them. They chose to call the building where they worshipped a meetinghouse rather than a church. They preferred Sabbath over Sunday, and they had no music with the singing of the Psalms.

Later they did use a pitch pipe, and somewhat later a tuning fork and a bass-viola, but it would be a long time, 1713 to be exact, before an organ was installed in a church in the Colonies.

Attendance at church or meetings was mandatory. Pilgrims punished those who missed services by placing them in the stocks on the meetinghouse grounds. Distance was no excuse, nor was time. They depended on a sundial outside and hourglasses inside, and a call from the church to attend services.

In those early days, they were summoned to church by drums, horns, or a shell. Some fired guns, but in many churches the drummer stood on the roof beating a drum. Another might blow a trumpet from the belfry or roof, while still another would summon worshippers by blowing a mournful sound on a conch shell.

The churches were extremely cold in winter and quite hot in summer. Fireplaces weren't built in the early churches, and it was many years before a stove was installed in most. That might have been the reason for the high-walled pews, spelled "pues" in the early days. The pews, complete with doors, must have been invaluable in keeping some of the cold air out. The ladies took their foot stoves filled with hot coals, while the men often took their dogs inside the pews. The dogs would lay on their feet, helping to keep them as warm as possible under those conditions. But it was still a chilly meeting at best.

The foot stoves were taken out during the "nooning" period and refilled with coals for the afternoon services. A fireplace supplied coal at the "noon-house" or tavern located near the church. Why the meetings were not held in these buildings during the most bitter part of the winter is unknown, but the worshippers did go to these buildings to eat their noon meal.

Not only were the meetinghouses or churches cold, but the services were unbelievably long. The morning and afternoon services usually lasted three to four hours, but five-hour sessions were not unusual. Some prayers were two hours long, but the average length was about an hour. Often the singing of a psalm required at least a half hour, especially if it had to be "lined and deaconed." To do this the deacon would read a line, then the congregation would sing it until the psalm was completed.

The worshippers stood during the singing of psalms and the prayers, which meant they could be standing for as much as four or five hours during the Sunday services. They were cold and often hungry, so they leaned against the walls of the pews for support.

Late sundial

Soapstone or potstone foot warmer might have been used in the carriage going to church

Fancy tin foot stove

Plain foot stove

The Puritans were sticklers for observing the Sabbath. They allowed no one to work or play. Even riding horseback was allowed only to church and back. Rulebreakers were punished with a fine and a whipping if the offense warranted it.

By the time churches were established in the southern Colonies, they were much more richly furnished. Each religious group—the Catholics in Maryland and parts of Virginia, the Quakers in Pennsylvania, the Baptists in Rhode Island, Episcopalians or the Church of England in Virginia and the Carolinas, and the Moravians in North Carolina—established their churches in the areas where the most members had established residence. They also made strict rules that were rigidly enforced.

The ladies wore black, "Sunday-go-to-meeting" dresses that, aside from white collars and cuffs, were very plain. By the 1800s, the colors were still on the dark side, but by this time women were wearing more browns, blues, and grays, and were often wearing them in the latest styles. Many families had become quite wealthy and many others could only be described as "well off," but all the wives were becoming style conscious. Magazines were beginning to be published picturing all the latest fashions from Paris. Heretofore women had had to depend on fashion dolls for their style changes.

Most women had a dressmaker who could copy the latest styles, and the ladies plunged headlong into a style-setting fervor. Remnants of that style-conscious era linger today. Styles changed and fads faded fast, yet the ladies continued to try to outdo each other in the fashion department.

Some poor housewives, usually those living on farms or in the rural areas, were unable to buy the fine materials to copy the Paris fashions, but they were ingenious. They often wove the fine fabrics on their old looms, and then made their dresses after the Paris fashions. They may not have been able to afford a fine hat, or even a cheap one, but she would make something out of what she had. Farm women were apt to make a hat using corn shucks.

Church rules relaxed through the years as the services became shorter. Eventually there was only the morning service. Rather than keep a group of small boys in one section where they were hard put to keep quiet and listen attentively to the services that lasted all day, they were allowed to play games in the afternoon, provided, of course, they had behaved properly during morning church services.

Young ladies were allowed to entertain "their young men" in the parlor on Sunday afternoon provided they only played the organ and sang church-related songs. Later they could entertain the young men by showing them views in the stereoscope or maybe looking at the trade and postcards assembled in a scrapbook.

Whereas ladies earlier had twisted their hair into tight little balls on top of their heads or at the nape of the neck, their descendants began to see their hair as their crowning glory. They not only began washing it more often, but they began rolling it on corn shucks at night hoping for curls the next day. A curl here and there looked much better when it escaped from a beribboned or flower-bedecked hat. Social events that didn't require a hat were few, but on those occasions women wore fancy combs in their hair.

Around the turn of the century, some of the ladies began cutting their hair. They began curling and waving it at home with an iron, some of which came with their own gas-burning heaters.

Infant's christening dress

Later hair comb

Bustles were stylish

Chairs like this were used in the wagon going to church and in the home the rest of the week

Bonnets and shawls worn by churchgoers around 1850

Around 1880, this was the favorite style for church

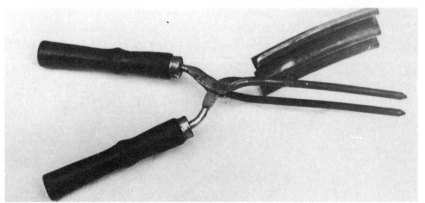

Iron was heated over the oil burning lamp to wave hair

*Churches were more than likely to have
this style of organ*

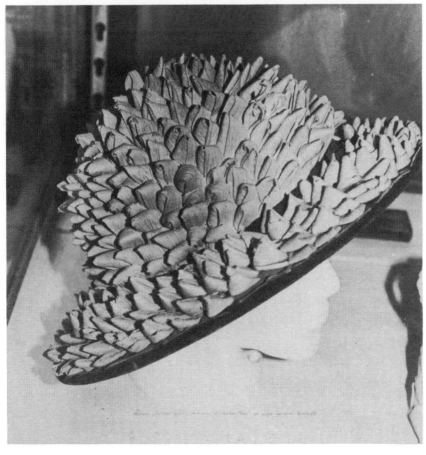

Hat made of corn shucks

This type of organ was more popular for home use

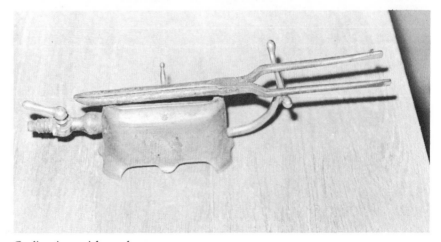

Curling iron with gas heater

In the beginning, women carried little or no money, so they had no use for handbags or purses. Later they carried a little black or brown leather handbag, often referred to as a reticule. By the turn of the century, they were carrying crocheted and beaded bags as well as small sterling silver ones. The Flapper chose mesh bags, sometimes with a small watch encased in the frame. The ladies were no longer wearing the small gold hunting case type watches on chains around their necks. Instead, they opted for the newly introduced wristwatch.

They had always worn a bit of jewelry, such as small opal earrings, a small pin with coral, or even a small handpainted pin. But those who could afford it had always worn the large brooches with precious stones. Cameos were a favorite with rich and poor alike.

Stereoscope

Round beaded bag

Mesh bag with watch in frame

Sterling silver bag

161

Lady's watch on handmade necklace made of hair from a horse's mane and tail

Cameo on crocheted choker

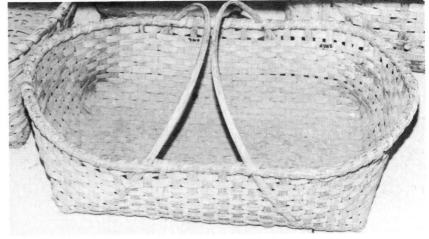

Basket used to take dinner to church

About the Author

All of her life the author has had a love affair with food. This in turn bred a familiarity and fondness for kitchens. Modern kitchens are marvelous, but she still prefers the warmth, tantalizing aromas, and comfort of the old kitchens. This explains why she often visits restorations, especially those with working kitchens. A favorite is the kitchen in the farmhouse at Westville, Georgia, where Vinnie is always cooking biscuits in a covered iron spider buried in coals on the hearth—biscuits that will later be served with ham or sausage. With new hot coals she will bake up a batch of heavenly tasting gingerbread. In fact, Vinnie says it is almost impossible to find a dish or food she can't prepare on the coals or on the crane in the large open fireplace. The ease and simplicity with which she prepares fireplace foods inspired Frances Thompson to begin this book.

The author now spends half of each year in Maine where she delves into the history of antiques in general and old kitchens in particular. The other half is spent in south Alabama checking southern cookery. "Some of the best-tasting," she says, "is still being done in open fireplaces and on woodburning stoves."

Price Guide

It is darn near impossible to assemble a price guide of more than a dozen items that reflects correctly the prices used in all parts of the country. Location, condition, supply, and demand all have a bearing on antique prices. A quick check of price tags on any identical or even similar items in a large show will prove the point sufficiently. It is extremely difficult to find two identical antiques or collectibles priced the same in adjoining booths or in shops on the same street.

One of the reasons is location. Few antiques enjoy the same popularity the country over. The only things that seem to be enjoying universal popularity right now are dolls and quilts. The rest have their areas of popularity. This difference is noticeable when studying auction reports. An item might bring top dollar in New York, while the same item wouldn't fetch one-third that amount in parts of the Sunbelt.

In order to determine an average price that serves as a guide regardless of location, prices were gathered from all sources, then averaged to arrive at one that would reflect today's asking prices for antiques from the kitchen.

Andirons, pair	
Blacksmith, plain	$19-45
Brass, small	150-175
Brass, large, c. 1800	250-300
Rabbit design	250-400
Hessian design	350-500
Antimacassar, crocheted	
Three-piece set	$55-75
Apple butter kettle	
Brass, large	$95-105
Brass, medium size	75-90
Brass, small	70-105
Apple butter stirrer	
Applewood, long handle	$25-35
Applewood, short handle	20-30
Apple dolls	
Princess	$30-45
Santa Claus	35-40
Warrior	25-35
Apple peelers	
Factory-made, plain, small	$35-50
Factory-made, large, fancy	60-85
Handmade wooden	90-105
Ash hopper	
V-shaped, wooden	$25-35
Bags/Purses	
Beaded, large	$65-80
Beaded, small	35-60
Mesh, plain	45-55
Mesh, watch in frame	90-125
Sterling	75-95
Barrels, wooden	
Handmade, wooden bands, medium	$60-70
Handmade, wooden bands, large	50-65
Baskets, woven splint	
Egg, depending on size and quality	$38-105
Laundry	55-65
Lunch, open	50-75
Miniature buttocks	40-70
Bathtubs	
Hip	$90-115
Plunge	135-150
Bean pots	
Iron, large	$23-35
Iron, small	17-30
Miniature	19-25
Beds, early handmade	
Baby	$245-300
Cherry, rope	850-950
Oak, plain	375-425
Poplar	700-800
Pine, rope	850-900
Trundle	500-600
Bed or rope key	
Homemade pine	$55-75
Bench	
Fireside, ornate	$750-850
Fireside, plain	300-500
Homemade for use at dining table	95-125
Bookmark	
Cross-stitch	$20-25
Boot scraper	
Old, with base	$55-75
Late, attached to step	45-55
Bowls, wooden	
Large, oval, maple	$40-50
Medium, Bird's-eye maple, oval	65-75
Small, late, oval	27-35
Large, round, maple	45-55
Medium, round, maple	40-50
Small, factory-made, round	12-20
Bread	
Board, round, wooden, "Bread" on edge	$32-37
Knife	17-22
Mixer or maker, c. 1914	40-55
Raiser or riser, tin	50-60

Buckets, water

Wooden, early, wooden bands	$55-60
Wooden, brass bands, late	40-50

Butter churns, complete

Brass	$135-150
Crock or stoneware	75-80
Daisy	40-50
Swinging	95-150
Wooden, handmade, wooden bands	145-165
Wooden, handmade, brass bands	125-140

Butter dishes

Cow design, old, glass	$105-125
Granite ware	50-75
Wee Branches pattern, glass, miniature	48-65

Butter ladles or scoops

Factory-made, early	$38-45
Handmade maple	75-85

Butter molds

Acorn design	$45-55
Cow design	200-225
Daisy	38-45
Pineapple	105-125
Shield	200-225
Star, small	29-40
Swan	175-200
Wheat	45-55
Large commercial-size mold	225-250
Hotel mold	75-85
Oblong, plain, late	30-35

Butter prints and stamps

Eagle	$200-225
Swan	135-150
Wheat	85-125

Cameo pin, 14K gold mounting

Portrait	$135-150
Scenic	195-225

Candleholders/Candlesticks (each)

Brass, tall	$65-85
Iron, early, blacksmith-made, tall	275-325
Iron, early, blacksmith-made, low	175-225
Pewter	105-145
Silver, plated	57-75
Silver, sterling	150-200
Miniature, brass, small	27-40
Miniature, brass, large	37-50

Candle molds

Three mold	$50-75
Eight mold	60-85
Twelve mold	75-90
Twenty-four molds, wooden frame	175-225

Candle snuffers

Iron	$24-40
Silver, plated, tray	66-75

Candy molds

Basket	$20-25
Corn	10-15
Fish	12-18
Santa Claus	35-40
Turkey	28-37

Centerpiece or doily

Crocheted border, fabric center	$28-35

Chairs

Brewster type, old	$2,500-3,000
Child's high chair, handmade	245-300
Hickory with cowhide bottom, straight	75-85
Shaker type, plain	200-250
Shaker type, rocker	300-350
Windsor type, comb back, handmade	1,200-1,500
Writing, movable arm	375-500

Cheese basket

Hexagon weave, large	$150-175

Cheese dish

Unmarked china	$150-165
Wedgwood	275-325

Cheese press

Homemade, wooden	$250-300

Cheese tester

Tin, wooden handle	$30-40

Cherry pitter or seeder

Clamp style, small	$45-50
Clamp style, large	60-75
Table-top model, old	55-65

Chests

Cedar, late	$185-215
English oak, early	1,900-2,250
Eighteenth-century walnut dower	6,500-8,000
Pennsylvania Dutch type	2,500-3,000
Pine, plain, handmade	450-600
Walnut, handmade, plain	900-1,100

Cider

Keg, handmade	$125-135
Mill	130-150
Press	98-125

Clothespins (dozen)

Wooden, regular size, c. 1910	$7-10
Wooden, toy size, c. 1901	10-15

Coffee mills

Glass, wall type	$25-39
Wooden, lap model, maple, maker's label	110-125
Wooden, lap model	74-85
Wall model, iron on wood base	36-55

Coffeepots

Cut glass	$3,000-3,500
Granite ware, gray, tin lid	40-50
Granite ware, pewter trim	235-250
Pewter, depending on age and quality	300-500

Combs, hair
Ornate	$60-65
Jeweled	85-95
Plain	35-40

Compote
Wooden, lathe turned	$25-35

Cookie Cutters, tin
Animals, late	$9-15
Hatchet, early, handmade	68-75
Heart, medium, early, handmade	45-60
Shoe, early handmade	65-75

Corn
Dryer, iron, early	$15-18
Grinder, Indian type	125-150
Grinder, pioneer type	135-150

Corner cupboards
Cherry, glass doors, refinished	$3,500-5,000
Cherry, solid doors, refinished	3,000-4,000
Hanging cupboard, small	500-750
Mixed woods, painted	1,400-2,000
Pine, excellent condition	2,450-3,500
Poplar, original	1,975-2,500
Walnut, glass doors, well made	3,150-3,750
Walnut, solid doors, rough	1,500-1,900

Cotton cards
Factory-made	$25-40

Cotton gin
Handmade	$65-75

Cradles
Hooded, fair workmanship	$225-350
Hooded, excellent workmanship	500-750
Low, small, handmade	250-300
Pennsylvania style	325-500
Swinging	225-450

Cranberry picker or scoop
Pine	$120-150

Creamers
Bullet-Emblem pattern, glass	$110-125
Cherry and Grape pattern, milk glass	55-65
China, applied leaves	35-45
Grape and Oval, miniature creamer and sugar	65-75
Scroll and Daisy pattern, glass	38-45

Cupboards
Cherry, handmade	$900-1,000
Maple, handmade	750-900
Mixed woods, handmade, poor quality	295-450
Oak, factory-made, plain	295-395
Oak, factory-made, ornate	595-750
Pine, handmade, plain	320-400
Pine, handmade, quality workmanship	675-850
Poplar	474-650
Walnut, handmade	950-1,200

Decanter
Imitation cut-glass pattern	$65-75

Decanter and wine set
Fickle Block pattern, miniature	$75-95

Desks
Child's	$115-125
Pine, handmade	400-550
Plantation, handmade, poor quality	275-350
Plantation, fine quality	1,000-1,200

Dough box
Original, without legs	$185-200
Cherry, with legs	495-575

Dough trays
Oblong, large, maple, handmade	$125-150
Oblong, medium, maple, factory-made	65-86
Oblong, small, maple, factory-made	55-75
Round, large, pine, handmade	115-125
Round, medium, maple, factory-made	55-75
Round, small, maple, handmade	75-85

Doughnut irons
Long handles	$75-95

Dresser or hutch
Oak, late	$575-750
English oak, early	2,250-3,000
Pine, handmade	950-1,200
Welsh type	1,750-2,500

Dryer, clothes
Wall hanging	$65-95

Dry sink
New England type, pine	$450-750
New England type, walnut	750-950
Southern country, small	215-350

Dutch oven, covered
Granite ware on iron	$75-85
Iron	40-50
Miniature iron	50-60

Eggbeaters
Regular size, old	$9-12
Toy size	12-15

Egg tester
Tin, one egg, experimental type	$75-85

Flax hatchel
Handmade	$59-75

Flax wheel
Small	$175-250
Large	150-175
Stand-up type	125-165

Food warmer, tin
Free-standing for fireplace	$165-175

Foot warmer
Soapstone	$50-60

Foot stoves, pierced tin
Well-made, good design	$175-195
Well-made, poor design	125-150

Fork, wooden

Late	$16-20

Frail

Handmade, early	$60-75

Game dishes and tureens

Game dishes, assorted styles, c. 1875	$140-150
Wedgwood tureen, early	350-400

Goblet

Portrait pattern, rare	$325-400

Granite ware

Miniature set cooking utensils	$550-750

Grate warmer

Tin container	$20-25

Graters

Corn, handmade	$35-45
Factory-made, medium size	18-25
Nutmeg, tin, early	39-45
Nutmeg, tin, medium	24-39
Nutmeg, table model	51-60

Hair irons

Curlers complete with gas heater	$31-40
Waving, lamp model	10-15

Ham boiler

Copper	$35-50

Hat, lady's

Corn shuck	$50-60

Honey press

Wooden, handmade, depending on quality	$150-250

Horn

Hunting horn to call dogs	$25-45
Powder horn made from cow's horn	33-47
Tumbler made from horn	21-35

Hunt board

Cherry	$8,000-9,500
Pine	3,750-4,500
Walnut	5,375-7,500

Iceboxes, oak

Two door, plain	$150-200
Two door, ornate	275-325
Three door, plain	225-250
Three door, ornate	495-600
Four door, ornate, mirror in door	695-750

Ice cream freezer

Wooden bucket	$69-75

Ice cream molds

Chicken	$20-27
Eagle	75-85
Train	50-60
Rabbit	25-35
Swan	45-55
Lamb	25-35

Ice cream scoop or disher

Early	$32-40
Late	10-12

Ice tongs

Small	$9-16
Large	17-24

Ink well

China	$95-105
Stoneware	35-40

Ironing boards, wooden

As found	$7-11
Decorated	45-50
Miniature	14-20

Irons

Charcoal	$36-40
Fluting, rocker type	27-35
Fluting machine	75-90
Gas	20-25
Gopher	52-60
Heater, patent date 1883	42-50
Heater, three matching irons	125-150
Milton Bradley Magic Plaiter	68-75
Mrs. Potts single iron with handle	28-35
Mrs. Potts, complete set of three	67-75
Pinking	23-30
Sadiron	9-12
Tailor's goose	34-40
Toy sadiron with trivet	25-35

Jelly cupboards

Glass panels in doors	$237-300
Pierced-tin door panels	450-600
Screen wire panels	195-275

Kitchen cabinets

Factory-made, late, ornate	$650-750
Factory-made, late, plain	195-235
Oak, handmade, early, quality	695-900
Oak, handmade, early, crude	165-200
Pine, handmade, early, quality	550-700
Pine, handmade, early, small	175-250

Knife tray

Factory-made, late	$23-40
Handmade, early, pine	85-95

Kraut cutters

Two-blade	$35-50
Three-blade	45-60
Four-blade	62-70

Lamps

Angle, single	$175-250
Betty	78-100
Grease	75-105
Iron, hanging, electrified	215-250

Lard squeezer

Wooden, handmade	$29-35

Lemon squeezers

All metal	$22-28
Combination metal and wood	34-40
All wooden	45-66

Lime squeezers

Metal	$10-15

Looms

Gallus	$130-150
Large for all types of weaving	350-450

Small	400-500
Ribbon	275-350

Meal chests

Maple, false front	$375-450
Pine, lift top	255-350

Milk cans, granite ware

Small, blue and white	$29-40
Medium, blue and white	38-50
Large, gray	42-55

Mortars and pestles

Brass, not too old	$75-95
Iron, blacksmith-made	97-115
Iron, factory-made	75-90
Stone	65-85
Wooden	105-135

Muffin pans

Iron, six muffins	$20-28
Iron, eleven muffins	39-47
Iron, twelve muffins	35-45
Tin, late, six muffins	15-20
Tin, late, twelve muffins	23-27
Cornsticks, iron, old	15-20
Vienna rolls, iron	36-40

Mugs

Mr. Pickwick	$95-125
Nursery rhyme, glass	37-50

Niddy noddy

All wood	$85-125

Nutcracker

Metal	$19-25
Wooden, small	14-20

Organs

Church type	$850-950
Parlor type	1,250-1,500

Pastry crimper

Early	$18-25
Late	9-12

Pie plate holder

Wire, six pies	$35-40

Pie safes

Cherry, pierced tin	$510-600
Oak, screen wire	215-275
Pine, pierced tin	390-475
Poplar, pierced tin	425-500
Walnut, pierced tin, unusual design	695-800

Piggin

Late	$77-90

Pitcher

Wooden, handmade	$135-150

Pitcher and tumblers, glass

Miniature Pattee Cross pattern	$75-85

Plates and chargers

Alphabet plate, child's	$55-60
Pewter charger, unmarked	175-250
Pewter charger, maker's mark	475-600
Pewter plate, unmarked	115-135
Pewter plate, maker's mark	400-900

Platters

Staffordshire, early	$225-250
Staffordshire, late	145-175
Wedgwood	275-350

Popcorn poppers

Tin	$23-28
Wire	15-20

Potato boiler/basket

Early	$65-75
Late	16-20

Potato slicer

Wooden, late	$17-24

Pudding or jelly molds

Granite ware	$67-75
Stoneware	47-55
Tin	35-40

Quilts

Appliqué, good quilting	$300-750
Appliqué, fine workmanship	350-1,000
Patchwork, fair, large pattern	150-275
Patchwork, excellent, small design	250-500
Crazy quilt, velvet, embroidery	200-350

Rattletrap/Noisemaker

Wooden, handmade	$125-150

Rolling pins

Glass, Nailsea type	$175-200
Glass, late, clear	17-20
Wooden, one piece, maple	28-35
Wooden, turning handles, maple	21-30
Wooden, hollow	30-37
Wooden, miniature	14-20

Salt boxes

Stoneware	$75-90
Wooden	77-95

Samplers

Early, good condition	$350-500
Late, good condition	150-200

Sausage mill

Metal, c. 1910	$35-40

Scales, brass front

Five pound	$25-35
Ten pound	46-50
Fifteen pound	30-35

Scrub board

Early wooden	$85-99

Shot glasses

Massachusetts pattern, state series	$35-40
Tarentum's Virginia pattern	24-30

Sieves, wooden frames

Fine wire	$27-35
Coarse wire	45-50

Skillets or spiders

Iron, long handle, legs	$35-45
Iron, miniature	17-25

Slaw cutters

All sizes	$18-20

Spice boxes	
Tin, round	$32-38
Wooden, standing, six-drawer	65-80
Wooden, standing, eight-drawer	85-97
Spinning wheels	
Maple	$195-225
Walnut	215-250
Spoons, wooden	
Advertising	$11-14
Candy, maple, handmade	24-30
Handmade, tiger maple	30-35
Slotted	19-23
Stereoscope	
Handheld	$50-75
Stoneware	
Crock, small	$75-85
Crock, medium, small decoration	250-300
Crock, large, decoration, advertising	500-750
Demijohn	78-105
Pitcher, maker unknown	175-300
Stoves, woodburning	
Cooking	$150-500
Granite ware	450-600
Heating, early	125-300
Strainers, tea	
Brass	$18-25
Silver, ornate	44-60
Wire, plain	13-17
Sugar chests	
Cherry	$5,000-6,500
Walnut	4,900-6,250
Sugar dishes	
Flint glass, c. 1840	$150-200
Staffordshire, early	100-125
Sundials	
Early	$275-300
Late	70-100
Swift	
Wooden	$95-125
Tables	
Butterfly, early	$875-2,000
Dropleaf, round	250-1,500
Round cherry, lazy Susan	500-2,500
Tavern, c. 1890	250-800
Trestle, old, good quality	850-1,600
Work	200-750
Teakettles	
Iron	$28-45
Granite ware	38-50
Granite ware on iron	48-75
Iron, miniature	37-45
Teapots	
Miniature Staffordshire, late	$95-125
Staffordshire, early	325-350
Tinware, late	
Cake pan, c. 1915	$8-12
Muffin pan, reworked, like new, c. 1915	22-31

Toasters	
Long-handled for fireplace	$20-25
Stove model, c. 1910	24-29
Towels	
Monogrammed	$45-50
Trenchers	
Wooden, handmade, old	$85-99
Trivet or gridiron	
Round, early	$145-200
Round, late	88-145
Tureen	
Gold band	$125-150
Haviland, miniature, holly design	65-75
Vase, wooden	
Factory-made, c. 1900	$15-20
Wafer irons	
Patent date 1880, iron	$75-95
Waffle irons	
Diamond design	$29-39
Heart and stars design	50-55
Washboards	
All wood	$65-75
Brass, wooden frame	25-45
Granite ware, blue, wooden frame	50-65
Miniature	25-30
Wooden rollers	85-95
Tin, wooden frame	18-22
Washing machines, early	
Copper tubs	$179-200
Wooden	158-175
Miniature, tin	39-50
Wash pots	
Iron	$50-65
Washtubs, wooden	
Large	$50-60
Medium	75-80
Small	65-70
Miniature	45-50
Watch, 18K gold hunting case	
Lady's	$325-400
Watch and horsehair necklace	650-750
Whetrock	
Small kitchen size	$15-20
Wines, glass	
Lincoln Drape pattern	$48-55
Wool cards	
Factory-made	$23-30
Wringer, wooden rollers	
Large	$27-35
Small	19-40
Miniature or toy size	30-38
Yarn winder	
Double spool	$300-325
Poplar, complete, original	175-200
Yoke, wooden	
Human or shoulder type	$86-98